The Frazzled Principal's Wellness Plan

D1314083

Slow Dance

Have you ever watched kids on a merry-go-round,
or listened to rain slapping the ground?
Ever followed a butterfly's erratic flight,
or gazed at the sun fading into the night?
You better slow down, don't dance so fast,
time is short, the music won't last.
Do you run through each day on the fly,
when you ask "How are you?", do you hear the reply?
When the day is done, do you lie in your bed,
with the next hundred chores running through
your head?
You better slow down, don't dance so fast
time is short, the music won't last.
Ever told your child, we'll do it tomorrow,
and in your haste, not see his sorrow?
Ever lost touch, let a friendship die?
'cause you never had time to call and say "hi"?
You better slow down, don't dance so fast,
time is short, the music won't last.
When you run so fast to get somewhere,
you miss half the fun of getting there.
When you worry and hurry through your day,
it's like an unopened gift thrown away.
Life isn't a race, so take it slower,
hear the music before your song is over.

David L. Weatherford
www.davidlweatherford.com

The Frazzled Principal's Wellness Plan

Reclaiming Time,
Managing Stress, and
Creating a Healthy Lifestyle

J. Allen Queen ★ Patsy S. Queen

CORWIN PRESS, INC.
A Sage Publications Company
Thousand Oaks, California

For information:

Corwin Press
A Sage Publications Company
2455 Teller Road
Thousand Oaks, California 91320
www.corwinpress.com

Sage Publications Ltd
1 Oliver's Yard
55 City Road
London EC1Y 1SP
United Kingdom

Sage Publications India Pvt. Ltd.
B-42, Panchsheel Enclave
Post Box 4109
New Delhi 110 017 India

Printed in the United States of America

Library of Congress Cataloging-in-Publication Data

Queen, J. Allen.
The frazzled principal's wellness plan : reclaiming time, managing stress, and creating a healthy lifestyle / J. Allen Queen and Patsy S. Queen.
    p. cm.
Includes bibliographical references and index.
ISBN 0-7619-8884-X (cloth) — ISBN 0-7619-8885-8 (pbk.)
    1. School principals—Health and hygiene—United States.
2. School principals—Time management—United States.
3. School principals—Job stress—United States. 4. Stress management—United States. I. Queen, Patsy S. II. Title. Title.
LB2831.958.Q44 2005
371.2′012—dc22

                                                    2004015948

This book is printed on acid-free paper.

05   06   07   08   09   10   9   8   7   6   5   4   3   2   1

Acquisitions Editor:	Faye Zucker
Production Editor:	Kristen Gibson
Copy Editor:	Diana Breti
Proofreader:	Ruth Saavedra
Typesetter:	C&M Digitals (P) Ltd.
Indexer:	Rick Hurd
Cover Designer:	Tracy E. Miller

Contents

List of Checklists and Planners

Physician's Foreword

The frazzled principal is the prototype of the frazzled American professional. Principals and district superintendents are, without a doubt, a special group of people who have accepted their responsibilities to help insure the education of America's future.

This book can help you, as an educational leader, to accomplish your work in the worst of situations and to be more effective in the best of situations. This program for time management gives all principals the tools to be as productive as your talents will allow you to be.

The Queens—Allen as an educational leader and Patsy as a nurse educator—have identified stress as a national epidemic. School administrator burnout is an American tragedy, and if the combination of stress and leadership are inevitable, your succumbing to that stress need not be. Understanding your stress, predicting your most vulnerable times, learning how to best cope—all are acquired skills that take practice. This book can help you. This book can change you. Allen and Patsy have made an educated study of the stresses educators face.

A majority of medical complaints can have their basis in stress. Physicians such as myself deal with stress-induced symptoms on a

---

Note: Dr. Schumacher is nationally known as a medical researcher and practitioner, a leader in the medical community, well-published in the literature of nutrition and obesity, and has appeared on several national television programs including ABC 20/20 and ABC Primetime. Dr. Schumacher was recently appointed Chairman of the Mecklenburg County Commissioners' Task Force for Healthy Weight in Children and Adolescents in Charlotte, North Carolina.

regular basis, and it is clear that stress can negatively affect your health. The authors discuss, in an insightful manner, the medical and psychological consequences of stress. Major points of healthy nutrition are outlined, and exercise is put into a practical and fun format.

As experienced professionals, the Queens are direct, sometimes critical of the education profession, and honest in their attempts to find answers for leaders working within an education system that includes rewards and sacrifices and disappointments. This book provides important preparation for educational leaders-in-training, helpful strategies for new principals, and a survival tool for seasoned veterans.

The Frazzled Principal's Wellness Plan is a book that weaves you through what you need to know, do, and avoid. The book begins with defining the unique stressors associated with leading a school or district. Allen and Patsy walk you through how to prepare for, to prevent, and to deal with school-related stress. You will be taught to identify and separate the good from the bad types of stress. This is a critical concept to grasp, and the Queens have it down.

The authors go on to show how to better balance your personal and professional lives by focusing on managing priorities. As a result, you should be able to maintain a healthier lifestyle, stay out of your doctor's office, and be your most effective self.

Self-assessment tools, coping skills and workbook sections are included. Exercise is always a must for stress relief, and their approaches are innovative and varied and there is definitely something for everyone. Exercise comes alive in this book. You will learn how to use your body and your mind for those times when immediate stress management is exactly what you need.

Doing a good job in leadership without ruining yourself in the process may be difficult if you are too much of a perfectionist or too much of a procrastinator. The Queens directly address these issues and give you options and time management strategies for all aspects of your work. They are quite frank in discussions about dealing with colleagues, superiors, and communication problems.

In the final section of this book, the Queens discuss the importance of balanced nutrition to help you be healthy and effective in life and in the school. Educators need a lot of help in this arena, and this section is all about habits, choices, snacks, and how to avoid temptations.

Donald Schumacher, M.D., Medical Director
Center for Nutrition and Preventive Medicine
Charlotte, North Carolina

Educator's Foreword

I am pleased to introduce and endorse Allen and Patsy's book, *The Frazzled Principal's Wellness Plan*, as the best guide on the topic that I have read. As a former elementary and secondary principal, I know firsthand the daily major stressors that impact school leaders. In Lincoln County Public Schools (NC), we are fortunate to have had Dr. Queen work with our principals directly, teaching them the valuable concepts of managing priorities, using time more effectively, and creating a healthy lifestyle.

Allen's long experience as a school principal, and his current role training principals as professor and chair of educational leadership at The University of North Carolina, Charlotte, give him great insight into problems that school leaders face on a daily basis. Patsy's experience and knowledge of nutrition and health as a nurse educator provide an excellent addition to this program. I say "program" because the book—with clearly written examples, insightful tools for self-analysis, wonderful photographs, and a generous selection of individual exercises from which to choose—provides the reader with a plan that goes beyond the parameters of what I expect in a book.

In our school system we are already using the Queens' companion book, *The Frazzled Teacher's Wellness Plan*. Principals and teacher leaders conduct sessions with faculty and staff members to do the stretching and Desktop Yoga activities. Emphasis on healthy nutritional choices and managing priorities in both personal and professional realms has had an impact on many of our employees. In fact, we are adding both books to our induction program as we strive to support and retain quality teachers, assistant principals, and newly appointed school principals. With the additional stress of federal and state mandates, we need every effective tool we can find to help our school principals and class-room teachers meet the new challenges of the 21st century.

I should add that many of the district office personnel are reading the books and practicing some of the easy-to-follow activities. I use several of Dr. Queen's breathing and Desktop Yoga activities in the privacy of my office for a few minutes each day. They help me lower my stress level prior to school board meetings and before dealing with parents. They calm me down each day before departing for home.

As a superintendent of a rapidly growing school system in a state requiring high-stakes testing, I recommend *The Frazzled Principal's Wellness Plan* to any principal, school leader, or district leader who wants to improve performance by learning to balance priorities, manage time and stress, gain vital skills, and create a healthy lifestyle.

Jim R. Watson, Superintendent
Lincoln County Public Schools
Lincolnton, North Carolina

Acknowledgments

W e would like to personally thank our editor, Faye Zucker, who inspired us to write this second book on a topic that consumes so much of our life. Our appreciation also goes to Stacy Wagner and to Julia Parnell for helping us to get this book into production. Special thanks to Tom Fisher who captured the essence of what we were trying to say in his wonderful cartoon drawings and to Diana Breti for her excellent copy editing work.

The content comes from much experience in classrooms and schools. We would like to thank our students, teachers, and graduate assistants who shared ideas and information about what needed to be included in this book. Special thanks to Brian, Deena, and Shala for your many hours of assistance.

Finally, we would like to thank Donald Shumacher and Jim Watson for their great forewords to this book. To have individuals of their caliber endorse our work with such kind words is an honor we will treasure forever.

Corwin Press thanks the following individuals for their contributions to this book:

Beverly C. Eidmann, Ed.D., Principal, Manzanita Elementary School, Newbury Park, CA

Donald Schumacher, M.D., Medical Director, Center for Nutrition and Preventive Medicine, Charlotte, North Carolina

Jim R. Watson, Ed.D., Superintendent, Lincoln County Public Schools, NC

For Mr. Charles Starnes, Principal, my senior year of high school
West Lincoln High School (1968–1969)
JAQ

About the Authors

J. Allen Queen is currently Professor and Chair of the Department of Educational Leadership at The University of North Carolina at Charlotte and has been a classroom teacher, principal, college administrator, and university professor. He has been a consultant to over 160 schools and districts in 36 states and 3 foreign countries in the areas of classroom discipline, school safety, block scheduling, and time management.

Dr. Queen has written over 20 books and 70 articles, including *The Frazzled Teacher's Wellness Plan* (Corwin Press, 2004) and books on karate for children. He holds the rank of Godan, Fifth Degree Black Belt in Shito-ryu Karate and learned the art and science of stress management from this sport. In addition, he has appeared on numerous radio and television programs, including ABC World News Now, and he can be seen presenting his de-frazzling strategies at schools in *The Frazzled Educator's Wellness Plan* produced by The LPD Video Journal of Education (TeachStream, 2004).

Dr. Queen enjoys working with teachers and principals in the areas of managing priorities, time management, and stress reduction. He has also worked with numerous universities, businesses, and government organizations in time and stress management. For several years he was a major consultant to the Justice Department in Washington, as a presenter of the Attorney General's Selective Seminars.

Dr. Queen is an annual presenter at several national conferences, and his favorite topic to present is Desktop Yoga, his creation.

 **Patsy S. Queen** holds a B.S. Ed. and a B.S.N from Western Carolina University and a M.S.N. from the University of Texas at Austin. In addition to nursing care positions in North Carolina, Virginia, and Texas, Patsy has 25 years' experience in nursing education. Currently an instructor at Gaston College, she has taught classes in adult health, maternal-child health, and nutrition.

Patsy has published articles in the *Journal of School Health* and the *Journal of Nursing Education.* She is co-author of *The Frazzled Teacher's Wellness Plan* (Corwin Press, 2004) and is currently working on a project on nursing assessment of the newborn (Elsevier, forthcoming). Patsy serves as an item writer for the National Council of State Boards of Nursing Registered Nurse (NCLEX-RN) Exam and the National Certification Corporation nursing specialty examination in Maternal-Infant Nursing.

 **Rose and Blanche Queen** are stress reduction consultants for the Queen family. Research about the human-animal health connection can be found at www.delta society.org

C H A P T E R   O N E

Educational Leadership in a Culture of Stress

Figure 1.1   Principals, superintendents, and other school leaders present a positive view to the public, but all of them work in situations that place great demands on their professional and personal priorities.

It's not that the job takes time . . . it's that it takes time doing things you don't want to be doing: state reports and things. We all want to give time to kids, but too much time is spent away from the kids.

John Young, *Chicago Tribune*, November 9, 2003

STRESS AND THE SCHOOL PRINCIPAL

With the daunting projection of 2.2 million teachers needed in the next decade, policymakers and the media have focused on our country's future need for qualified teachers; however, an equally important issue that must be addressed is that of school leadership (Educational Research Service, 1998; Keithwood & Prestine, 2002; Kochan, Riehl, & Bredeson, 2002; Lugg, Bulkey, Firestone, & Garner, 2002; Pounder, Reitzug, & Young, 2002; Spillane & Louis, 2002).

While the debate continues about a current versus a pending shortage of principals (Educational Research Service, 1998; NAESP, 1990; Peterson & Kelley, 2001; Steinberg, 2000; Stricherz, 2001), it is obvious that there is growing concern that time and stress management problems for principals have increased to the point that many qualified individuals do not want to become school leaders. Facing "numerous evenings and weekends at schools, watching extracurricular activities and attending meetings . . . the long hours, the difficulty of meeting underfunded mandates such as the No Child Left Behind Act," principals keep retiring on schedule, many schools are left without principals, and school systems are having difficulty replacing "a graying corps of principals at a time when the pressure to raise test scores and other new demands have made an already difficult job an increasingly thankless one" (Steinberg, 2000).

Ferrandino (2001) cites a plethora of reasons for the shortage of new principals: inadequate compensation, job-related stress, and time commitment issues. Of major concern also is the tremendous pressure on principals to meet state-mandated standards, with accountability pressures continuing to increase as a result of the *No Child Left Behind Act* of 2001 (NCLB). States are required to create strong standards for what every student should know and learn in grades 3–8, with NCLB further requiring school districts to close the achievement gap between students and improve school safety, character education, and teacher preparation. Thus the principal's role now requires instructional leadership, community leadership, and systems management to ensure the success of all students (Ferrandino, 2001; Furman & Starratt, 2002; Goldring & Greenfield, 2002; Murphy & Louis, 1999; Peterson & Kelley, 2001; Rowan, 1995; Wallace, 1996).

One characteristic evident in high-performing schools is a dedicated and dynamic principal. Strong leadership is essential for effective school reform (Goldring & Rallis, 1993; Murphy, 2002a, 2002b; Murphy & Louis, 1999; Wallace, 1996). That means we must address the factors causing qualified individuals to turn away from the principalship. In their report *Preparing a New Breed of School Principals: It's Time for Action*, Bottoms and O'Neill (2001) have started the "battle cry" to change the school environment, which today can easily be labeled a culture of stress.

STRESS AND CENTRAL OFFICE PERSONNEL

The culture of stress is not limited to the principal in individual school buildings. Often the entire school system can be a culture of stress, and sometimes the stress starts at the central office level. Superintendents, including associate and assistant superintendents, directors, and supervisors, all work in situations that place great demands on their professional and personal priorities. As with principals, superintendents and central office personnel do well in presenting a positive view to the public, and, in fact, most are positive about what they are trying to accomplish. However, in personnel meetings and in private meetings, often the anger, frustration, and related stress can become obvious.

In research presented at the annual meeting of the University Council for Education Administration, Richardson (1999) reported that the superintendents she studied identified the following as their major sources of stress: relationship with the school board, heavy workload demands, public demands and politics, state and federal mandates, and personnel issues. Richardson further elaborated that these major sources of stress have "significant impact on superintendents' personal and professional lives and engender a range of negative feelings" (p. 14), including feeling isolated and, often, powerless.

As with principals, stress has an impact on whether superintendents remain in their jobs. In a 2001 study conducted with over 250 superintendents in Texas, Lowery et al. reported that job expectations have become unrealistic and that educators are less interested in the top role. While there are positive reasons for becoming and remaining a superintendent, negative factors include politics, high demands, and stress (Lowery, Harris, Hopson, & Marshall, 2001). From the abundant literature and from direct observations, we can therefore conclude that although responsibilities and demands may vary from the central office to the individual school level, superintendents, associate and assistant superintendents, directors, and supervisors all experience high levels of stress, much as we find with principals and assistant principals.

LIFE EVENTS AND WORKPLACE STRESS

Personal Stressors

Traditionally, students bring distractions and stressors from outside the classroom setting ("life events") with them to school every day. Principals also have to deal with life event stressors and "social baggage" that teachers bring to school. Principals cannot and should not be required to deal with family problems, street life, or community problems, but often the principal—especially the elementary principal—has to serve in multiple roles, from nurse to counselor.

The principal's personal stressors are also at work during the day: car accident, illness of a family member, divorce, debt, trouble with in-laws, changes in living conditions, financial situations,

Research Note: Life Events and Stress

One study of stressful life events focused on events that occurred to more than half the students in each school studied. The researchers identified three life events that were present in the top six for every school: (1) death of a close friend or relative, (2) money problems experienced by the family, and (3) change in relationships with "people you know" (Plunkett, Radmacher, & Moll-Phanara, 2000). When students are stressed and upset, their behavior usually deteriorates, with teacher and principal stress levels increasing proportionally. Principals also have to deal with the life event stressors that teachers bring to school.

death of a loved one. Even though personal stressors were not created in school, each stressor still may affect a principal's overall performance.

Non-Instructional Responsibilities

Handling discipline problems; dealing with gangs and school violence; completing excessive paperwork; attending too many meetings in and away from school; and implementing constantly changing federal, state, and local mandates are viewed as detriments to instructional leadership by most school principals. Also on this list: dealing with irate parents and trying to survive in a high-stakes testing environment. These are managerial tasks, but when they occupy most of the time the principal needs to spend on instructional leadership, they can and do trigger stress.

Other stressors come from feeling harassed by superiors, from fielding too many complaints from teachers about additional assignments or lack of support, or from fears of increasing teacher absenteeism and a dwindling pool of capable substitutes. Each of these stressors not only affects the principal's health but can also flow negatively toward faculty, staff, and even students.

> Research Note: Role Uncertainty
> High levels of anxiety may be created by increased demands or a greater degree of role uncertainty. A principal's ability to make decisions may be impaired when ability to concentrate is reduced. Principals may experience a feeling of panic or a sharp loss of confidence in leadership ability. With prolonged exposure to the anxiety of role uncertainty, principals may reach an exhaustion threshold, commonly described as feeling "drained."

Finding and Keeping Qualified Teachers

Many principals work 10–15 hours per day during the summer trying to find teachers to fill open positions. Still, many schools in the United States start September with vacant positions.

Principals are stressed when teachers are stressed. Most new teachers enter the ranks with enthusiasm, but more than 20%

of them leave the profession within the first three years, with predictions showing that 50% will leave after five years and 80% after ten years (Boreen & Niday, 2000; Gold, Thornton, & Metules, 2001; Queen, 2002; Streisand & Tote, 1998). It is also our experience that a much greater number of today's teacher education graduates awarded teaching licensure or credentials do not go into teaching. Many teachers are lured by businesses and industries promising higher salaries and better benefits, a healthier work environment, and lower levels of job stress. This phenomenon, in combination with the demographic of more than one half of practicing teachers reaching retirement age within the next five to ten years, means that schools are experiencing growing teacher shortages at just about every level and in every subject area.

Principals who accept nonqualified teachers—those who are changing careers or rebounding from corporate and government downsizing—often find stress levels increasing once those teachers reach the classroom and discover the stigma that "anybody can teach" is a false and frightening claim. Unprepared to teach specific content areas, or lacking basic teaching skills, many of these recruits may not be willing to work through the early and largely overwhelming "hands-on" induction and training programs necessary to get them through their first year in the classroom (Boreen & Niday, 2000; Gold, Thornton, & Metules, 2001; Queen, 2002; Streisand & Tote, 1998).

School Reform

Always complicating workplace stress is the assumption of school reformers that teachers, principals, and central office personnel are the problem and the reason for mediocre school performance. Teacher and principal "bashing," "teacher-proof" instructional reforms, and mandatory reports of "annual yearly progress" are all signs that the wrongs of education and even society are being attributed to incompetent, inconsiderate, and self-serving teachers, principals, and administrators (Glickman, Gordon, & Ross-Gordon, 2001; Queen, 2002). That is truly a culture of stress.

Research Note: Finding and Keeping Qualified Teachers

According to the 2003 Kappan Gallup Poll, the public believes that getting (75%) and keeping (87%) good teachers are both problems for the schools. The researchers compared these findings to 1969 when respondents rated getting (52%) and keeping (42%) good teachers as problems. In a related question, 45% of parents with children in schools gave the local schools where their children attended a grade of C or lower, compared to 55% of individuals without children. A large percentage (70%) of the public who responded to the survey knew "from a fair amount to nothing at all" about the *No Child Left Behind Act* of 2001. This is a stressful point for principals in that it is becoming more difficult to get and keep good teachers, and it will become even a greater problem because NCLB requires that every classroom be staffed with a teacher who is certified or licensed by the 2005–2006 school year.

To learn more about the *No Child Left Behind Act* of 2001, visit www.ed.gov/nclb/landing.jhtml.

To learn more about teacher training, visit The National Council for Accreditation of Teacher Education at www.ncate.org.

STRESS AND THE IMMUNE SYSTEM

What happens in a culture of stress? A *culture* may be defined as a pattern of beliefs, values, and practices, shared by a group or organization. Culture basically defines how things are done. *Stress*, clinically defined, is the sum of the biological reactions to any adverse stimulus, mental or emotional, internal or external, that tends to disturb the organism's balance or homeostasis. And leadership *burnout*, whether it affects principals, superintendents, or other leaders, can be viewed as a state of chronic stress—physical, emotional, and mental exhaustion resulting from an inability to cope effectively with the daily stresses of leadership over an extended period of time. Generally, people under stress can be irritable, anxious, angry, or sad, but chronic stress may lead to immune responses that cause severe problems throughout the body.

Research Note: Stress and Your Health

The immune system's connection to bodily systems results in a significant correlation between stress and health, with negative stress linked to psychological, cardiovascular, respiratory, and physical trauma. Psychological and somatic complaints by principals include fatigue and weakness, blurred vision, irritability, sensitivity to weather, dizziness, malaise, and depression. Dysfunctional cardiovascular systems may cause palpitations, hypertension, arteriosclerosis, and coronary artery disease. Stress on the musculoskeletal system can cause back difficulties, cervical tension, and headaches. Respiratory system dysfunctions include repeated upper respiratory infections, bronchial asthma, and hyperventilation. Lastly, physical trauma may include lacerations, bruises, head injuries, seizures, and deafness.

The Immune Response

When it works correctly, the immune system controls our defenses against infectious disease by attacking foreign substances that are not naturally part of the body. Not confined to one organ or one site in the body, the immune system is everywhere, providing an assortment of specialized cells that occupy the skin, eyes, nostrils, lungs, and the lining of internal organs.

When a part of the body gives a "distress" call, the immune cells charge to the problem area by route of the lymphatic system. Thus acute stress activates the immune system. Many health professionals use the term "distress" to identify stress that is considered negative and to differentiate it from stress that is considered positive. But even positive stress can cause problems if not balanced. Think of the holiday season, a wedding, or the birth of a child. The body really does not know the difference and attempts to return to a state of balance and homeostasis as quickly as possible.

Acute Stress

The body reacts each time it encounters a stressor. There are three basic stages in the stress response:

- Stage 1, Alarm, refers to the body mobilizing for "fight or flight."
- Stage 2, Resistance, in which the individual combats the stressor. Through purposeful action, the individual attempts to reduce the stressor by using coping tactics.
- Stage 3, Exhaustion, in which unrelieved stress can turn into burnout.

The immune response causes changes within the body. Adrenaline starts to flow throughout the body. The heart rate begins to accelerate. An increase in blood pressure and blood clotting occurs. And while these other body functions are speeding up, the digestion system slows down.

Aspects of immune function may be bolstered by bursts of short-term stress. But when stressful situations become chronic, the immune system may falter and health problems may follow.

> **Research Note: Viral Infections**
> Studies have shown individuals who tend to be unhappy, measured by psychological testing, were more likely to have recurrent cold sores. Higher levels of antibodies to herpes viruses were common in people under various kinds of stress. High antibodies to herpes indicate a sign of low immune function. Consistent and convincing evidence shows that stress can affect the body's control over herpes virus infections.

Chronic and Prolonged Stress

According to researchers in psychoneuroimmunology (PNI), prolonged stress can lead to a decrease in immune function, and excessive immune system activity can lead to autoimmune disease, whereby immune system antibodies mistakenly identify the body's healthy cells as foreign invaders and attack. Life-threatening organ damage and chronic inflammation can then cause psychological, cardiovascular, respiratory, and physical traumas. Stress even reduces our resistance to bacteria and viruses, making us more susceptible to the common cold.

Psychological and somatic symptoms of chronic stress may include fatigue and weakness, blurred vision, irritability, sensitivity to weather, dizziness, headaches, insomnia, upset stomach, chronic back pain, skin rash, menstrual problems, malaise, and depression. Autoimmune disorders linked to chronic stress include rheumatoid arthritis, systemic lupus erythematosus (SLE), and type 1 diabetes.

If exhaustion levels are not relieved once acute stress has transformed to chronic stress, burnout follows. Principals who reach the burnout stage usually are completely drained emotionally, physically, behaviorally, mentally, sexually, and spiritually.

Burnout

While all educational leaders are subject to high levels of stress and burnout, we believe that leaders in the principalship, often termed an "undoable position," are major candidates for burnout. With today's abundance of chronic stressors—dealing with teachers over state versus local curriculum standards, controlling inappropriate student behavior, reinforcing the importance of reaching school test goals, calming irate parents, attending numerous meetings, working with budget issues, and writing reports—it does not take long for today's principal to reach the state of exhaustion known as burnout. There are conflicting reports, but something like 50% to 75% of principals view educational leadership at the school level as the most stressful job in education.

> To Learn More . . .
> Visit www.niaid.nih.gov and www.webdoctor.com to learn more about how the immune system works.

In other words, as an educational leader you can become sick in a school building or district office that is stressful. And all school buildings and central offices are stressful. Therefore, *you have two choices:*

- Use precautions or plan activities to prevent or eliminate the adverse stimuli, or
- If unpreventable, you must counteract the adversity to reach life balance or return to a state of homeostasis.

Figure 1.2   Principals can bring stress reduction activities to their school, including group meditation as shown here. Other activities include relaxation training, physical exercise, health and wellness programs, and time management seminars.

REDEFINING THE CULTURE OF STRESS FROM A HEALTHIER PERSPECTIVE

High demands in a changing society will continue to cause great stress for educational leaders. It is imperative that all school leaders begin to examine the effects of the culture of stress so they can begin the process of reclaiming their time, priorities, and good health.

Educational leaders should not work alone when managing the culture of stress in a school or district. From the central office to the school office, each leader can and should specify and clarify prescribed roles and expectations so that subordinates can operate within those roles most effectively. This also means that school

Figure 1.3   Principals and teachers can work together to reduce stress at school and in the classroom. Good strategies for principals include seeking input in goal setting and decision making, providing social support time for faculty and staff, and developing settings that promote superior mentor/mentee relationships.

boards can and should ensure that the workload is appropriate for superintendents.

In the school building, we have found two main strategies whereby principals can help change the culture of stress. The first is by helping to manage reactions to stress, both for themselves and their colleagues and staff. Principals can bring relaxation training, opportunities for physical exercise, health and wellness programs, and time management seminars to their schools, and all of these are activities that *the principal should attend* (see Figure 1.2).

Second, principals need to think about how their administrative actions may be creating unnecessary sources of stress. Setting unrealistic deadlines for the completion of tasks and failing to communicate adequately give rise to avoidable problems. Instead principals should aim to establish clear guidelines and responsibilities;

seek input in goal setting and decision making; provide social support time for faculty and staff; and develop settings that promote superior mentor/mentee relationships. Principals can make great partners and can learn with teachers as they provide these services. Principals and teachers can work together to reduce stress at school and in the classroom (see Figure 1.3).

Systems of social support are essential for managing stress. Even something as simple as sharing problems, exchanging solutions, or engaging in social activity with colleagues can help dissipate feelings of stress and turn them into the feeling that "We are in this *together*."

Chapter Two

Restructuring Personal and Leadership Priorities for a Healthy Lifestyle

Figure 2.1 Work, work, work.

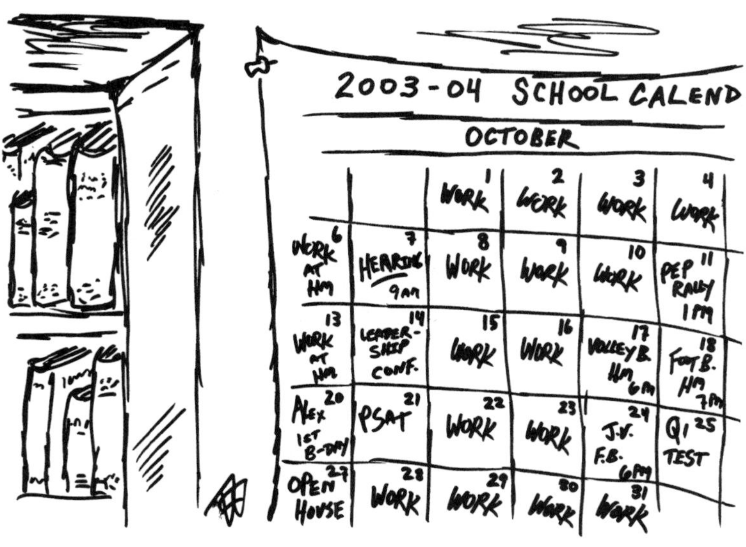

> *Balancing work and personal life that benefits organizations and individual employees, managers are guided by three principles: (1) clarify what is important; (2) support employees as whole people; and (3) experiment with how work is done to enhance the organization's performance while creating time and energy for employees' personal pursuits.*

> Friedman, Christensen, & DeGroot, 1998

WHY MANAGE PRIORITIES?

Assume that a major catastrophe has just occurred or is in progress. It may be your house on fire, an automobile accident, or a plane crash. In 30 seconds, write down three things that come immediately to mind.

1.

2.

3.

Probably, if you are honest with yourself, most of the items that you listed are related to your spouse or significant other, children, family members or friends, and perhaps spiritual or deeply personal thoughts. As you may have heard before, people who are terminally ill do not think about the things left undone at work or related professional concerns.

If you are like most principals, however, you are constantly thinking about lesson plans, problem students, deadlines, reports, and budgets. It is truly amazing how we can change our thought patterns when serious situations occur. In actuality, the items you listed above probably are the *real* priorities in your life. But due to stress, lack of time, and the ability to do the wrong things well, your real priorities may very well be neglected on a daily basis. Think about it!

So why manage priorities? Simply to give yourself more personal time to do the things that you want to do, and to lower your stress level.

IDENTIFYING YOUR PRIORITIES

Meet Lloyd and Leslie: Sound Familiar?

Lloyd, an elementary principal, loves to bike. However, due to conflicting schedules, he never seems to find the time. Even when he gets to go biking, he finds his thoughts returning to tasks left incomplete on his desk at school. Lloyd is suffering from *priority guilt*. He is preoccupied with thoughts of leadership responsibilities and becomes anxiety-ridden and stressed, thus failing to enjoy the present moments.

Leslie, a new supervisor in central office, is thrilled about her new position, but she soon discovers that the hours she has always reserved just for herself for reading, walking, and other relaxing activities she enjoys are now gone. She notices an increase in her anxiety level and faces the demands of her new job in less than a positive manner.

Balancing Professional and Personal Priorities

As educational leaders, Lloyd and Leslie are putting more of their personal time and energy into their leadership priorities. These priorities are in constant competition with their personal priorities. If you have leadership priorities and personal priorities that are in continuous competition, the next activity (Checklists 2.1 and 2.2) will help you to set up a program to balance professional and personal priorities. You begin determining priorities, both professionally and personally, by identifying problem areas. If you can't identify what your problems are, then you will probably solve the wrong problems.

Checklist 2.1

Identifying Your Personal and
Professional Priorities: Problem Analysis I

Examine each item that follows and rate yourself by completing the sentence with Usually (mark with the letter A), Sometimes (mark with the letter B), or Seldom (mark with the letter C). We strongly recommend that you have a close family member and a professional colleague rate you in the same areas so you can compare their perceptions with your own. The closer their ratings are to yours, the better your assessment of what is really happening in your life. Be sure to ask individuals who will be *honest and fair* to you in their ratings.

Example: From my perception, I	**Usually**	**Sometimes**	**Seldom**
1. Have enough time for myself.		B	

From my perception, I	Usually	Sometimes	Seldom
1. Have enough time for myself.			
2. Have enough time for my family.			
3. Have enough time for responsibilities at work.			
4. Have a clear understanding of ALL my priorities.			
5. Set long-range and short-range goals.			
6. Achieve my leadership goals.			
7. Maintain a high level of energy.			
8. Maintain a high level of enthusiasm.			
9. Am motivated to do my best at work.			
10. Avoid postponing difficult or unpleasant tasks.			
11. Consolidate activities at home.			
12. Keep a place for everything.			
13. Manage change effectively, personally and professionally.			

14. Can say "no" easily and tactfully, even to my superior. _____ _____ _____

15. Use time wisely in the office and personally. _____ _____ _____

16. Allow other people to use their time appropriately. _____ _____ _____

17. Control interruptions from my planned duties. _____ _____ _____

18. Avoid taking on too many responsibilities, especially at school/district. _____ _____ _____

19. Avoid taking on too many responsibilities with my family/friends. _____ _____ _____

20. Coordinate work with others. _____ _____ _____

21. Delegate responsibilities responsibly to family members. _____ _____ _____

22. Communicate well with colleagues and superiors. _____ _____ _____

23. Listen while others talk, especially teachers. _____ _____ _____

24. Maintain a high level of written communication skills. _____ _____ _____

25. Manage totally unexpected change effectively. _____ _____ _____

26. Manage well in crisis situations at home and school/district. _____ _____ _____

27. Prioritize my personal interests. _____ _____ _____

28. Review personal goals periodically. _____ _____ _____

29. Keep a personal
     daily, weekly, monthly,
     and yearly plan.   _____   _____   _____

30. Acknowledge
     personal and
     leadership weaknesses.   _____   _____   _____

Checklist 2.2

*Analyzing Your Personal and
Professional Priorities: Problem Analysis I*

You may notice that the statements in Checklist 2.1 covered both personal and leadership situations. Re-examine the 30 statements. For any statement that you marked with a C (Seldom), list that problem below as personal, leadership, or both.

Problem Analysis I for Personal Priorities

1. _____
2. _____
3. _____
4. _____
5. _____
6. _____
7. _____
8. _____

Problem Analysis I for Leadership Priorities

1. _____
2. _____
3. _____

4. _____

5. _____

6. _____

7. _____

8. _____

Problem Analysis I for *both* Personal and Leadership Priorities

1. _____

2. _____

3. _____

4. _____

Next, examine each category closely

1. Do you see any item that is listed in both personal and leadership?

2. How do your ratings compare with those of your family member or colleague?

3. Analyze which of the items under Personal and Leadership cause you the most frustration. As previously stated, it is important to see how family and colleagues may have rated you (if you chose to include that in the activity), but it is now time for YOU to further analyze the categories for the items that cause you the most frustration or stress and to organize these in *priority* order, with the most frustrating or stressful one becoming priority number 1.

My Priority Order of Frustrations and Stress

We suggest that you write these out.

Personal

1. _____

2. _____

3. _____

4. _____

5. _____

Leadership

1. _____

2. _____

3. _____

4. _____

5. _____

Meet Christopher, A New Assistant Principal

Christopher is new to school leadership. He had been in the business world for almost 20 years before his company downsized and he lost his job. He and his wife have two teenage children at home, and he decided to try teaching. Entering the profession as a lateral-entry business teacher while working on his teaching certificate, he found much success in the classroom. Several principals encouraged him to go into school leadership.

After four years of teaching, Christopher went back to school at night for four more years and received his master's degree in school administration. While the process was stressful, he was able to balance teaching, graduate school, marriage, and fatherhood. But once he started in his new position as Assistant Principal, Christopher soon experienced many stressful situations. When his duties suddenly tripled, he noticed dramatic increases in stress and frustration. In addition, his children are now older and their social lives are taking larger amounts of time away from home and family responsibilities. Not wanting to cause friction at his new job or at home, Christopher fails to be assertive and assumes greater numbers of tasks and responsibilities. When Christopher completes his Problem Analysis I activity, he realizes that he has a problem with numbers 2, 3, 8, 10, 11, 18, 19, 20, and 30 in his personal and leadership lives. His next step is to list *in order of priority* the areas in which he sees the most frustrating or stressful problems.

Christopher's Problem Analysis I

Here is Christopher's list of the problem items in his personal life:

1. Avoid taking on too many responsibilities with my family/ friends (Item 19)

2. Have enough time for my family (Item 2)

3. Consolidate activities at home (Item 11)

4. Avoid postponing difficult or unpleasant tasks (Item 10)

5. Coordinate work with others (Item 20)

Here is Christopher's list of the problem items in his school leadership life:

1. Acknowledge personal and leadership weaknesses (Item 30)

2. Avoid taking on too many responsibilities, especially at school/district (Item 18)

3. Avoid postponing difficult or unpleasant tasks (Item 18)

4. Have enough time for responsibilities at school/district (Item 3)

5. Maintain a high level of enthusiasm (Item 8)

As can be observed, Christopher had many of the same items in each list but in a different priority. As you completed your Problem Analysis I, you may have discovered a similar pattern or a totally different one. The important task is to determine your needs. If you have fewer than ten problem areas, super—but try not to list more than five items in each area.

YOUR MIRROR IMAGE OF SELF

Once you have determined your basic need areas, it is time for a closer examination of self. Five major components make up a *mirror image of self*: physical, emotional, intellectual, professional, and social. Every event, item, or activity in your life is related to one or more of these items. You should be aware that millions of individuals pay exorbitant amounts of money annually to determine problem areas. Of course, nothing replaces getting a complete physical examination, but probably you are aware if you are physically fit. In addition, you know your basic intelligence level, your sociability, and your emotional stability. Problem Analysis II (Checklist 2.3) is a fun, but important, activity to determine problems and begin a plan for improvement.

Checklist 2.3

Your Mirror Image of Self: Problem Analysis II

Please complete the following statements.

Physically

I am _____

I can _____

I need _____

I will _____

Emotionally

I am _____

I can _____

I need _____

I will _____

Intellectually

I am _____

I can _____

I need _____

I will _____

Professionally

I am _____

I can _____

I need _____

I will _____

Socially

I am _____

I can _____

I need _____

I will _____

Meet Wendy, A High School Principal

Wendy, a high school principal, has entered into her middle thirties. During her college years, she remained trim, energetic, and healthy. As a classroom teacher she continued to watch her diet and health. Then she became a principal. Overnight, as her duties and responsibilities at school increased, so did her eating. In addition to carrying 30 pounds of extra weight, she seldom exercised and felt depressed because the offers for an evening out were fewer than she received 10 years ago. Her afternoons and evenings were filled with additional time in the school office, school activities, or events. Once a voracious reader, Wendy did not have the energy or take the time to venture into new books or intellectual activities. As Wendy sat down to complete the mirror image of self activity, she was shocked into the realization that her problems had gotten out of hand. Thus her analysis was as follows:

Physically

I **am** 30 pounds overweight and out of shape.

I **can** lose the excess weight and get in shape.

I **need** to get a physical and begin a diet and exercise program.

I **will** make the appointment for the physical examination immediately and begin the recommended diet and exercise programs as supervised.

Emotionally

I **am** finding myself smiling less these days.

I **can** smile more.

I **need** to smile more and view things positively.

I **will** purchase a self-help book or see a professional for help.

Intellectually

I **am** of above-average intelligence.

I **can** discuss numerous topics.

I **need** to read more often.

I **will** visit the library once a week.

Professionally

I **am** a competent and an effective principal.

I **can** guide my teachers effectively in instruction and classroom management.

I **need** to find an effective way to manage my weekly agenda and lower my stress level.

I **will** effectively manage my weekly agenda and lower my stress level at school.

Socially

I **am** growing more and more unsociable.

I **can** see myself becoming more distant with my friends.

I **need** to be more sociable, open, and relaxed.

I **will** find a method to relax so I can become more sociable.

By being honest and conducting an informal analysis of herself, Wendy was ready to begin the process of improvement with a focus on her problem areas. Now it is time for you to complete your activity analysis in the five areas. Nobody else has to

Research Note: Perceived Priorities vs. Actual Priorities

In a recent survey of school principals, Whitaker and Turner (2000) found that disparities exist among rankings of perceived priorities and actual priorities. Several important conclusions emerged from their study:

- Principals felt that all the responsibilities of their jobs are important.
- No matter how much principals actually emphasized a task, they felt that they should be doing even more in that area.
- School climate was the highest priority among principals.
- Principals recognized the need for improving their time management.
- The numerous responsibilities of principals make the job tremendously stressful.

The authors recommended that principals focus on the priorities they could control; develop, refine, and improve their time management skills; and recognize which tasks principals must do and which tasks can be shared or delegated, which would not only reduce stress for the principals but would also empower their staff members.

see your evaluation. This is for your improvement, so be honest and direct.

MAKING PRIORITIES YOUR PERSONAL MISSION

Thus far you have examined the concept of managing priorities and analyzed some problems you face personally and in leadership. To be an effective educational leader, you must know how to manage priorities with your superiors, faculty, colleagues, family, and *yourself.* Use Checklist 2.4 to continue your Problem Analysis II.

Checklist 2.4

*Making Priorities Your
Personal Mission: Problem Analysis II*

Examine and respond to the following:

1. How can your personal life influence your leadership?

_____

_____

_____

2. To be the best educational leader I can, I must be

A. _____

B. _____

C. _____

D. _____

E. _____

In question 1, you may have responded by stating that both spheres of your life influence each other, and it is difficult to completely separate personal and professional personalities. And, usually, if you are a demanding, driven, high-expectations type of person in your personal life, you will have a similar style of managing or working with students and colleagues. Conversely, if you are unorganized, careless, or unconcerned personally, you probably will have a similar attitude professionally.

In question 2, you may very well have listed such qualities as highly competent, dedicated, organized, energetic, flexible, honest, fair, and so on. That confirms that you are on target with the attributes of an excellent principal.

Now that you have determined your priorities, it is time to examine methods you can use to find the appropriate time to implement your priorities and to better manage stress in your life.

CHAPTER THREE

Mastering the Science of Stress Management for Better Health

Figure 3.1   Stress prevention is your best bet, but prevention often doesn't work with school boards. That's when you need to turn to strategies for stress *reduction*.

FACTORS INFLUENCING STRESS LEVELS

Coping Strategies

Principals can do many things to manage and reduce stress. Individual coping strategies fall into two main categories: direct action techniques and palliative techniques.

Direct vs. Palliative Strategies. Principals who use direct action techniques learn to reduce or eliminate stress by first getting a clear idea as to its source. The principal then reduces or prevents stress by changing the source or situation in some way to prevent triggering stress in the future. Direct action techniques may involve managing or organizing oneself more effectively; developing new knowledge, skills, and working practices; or even negotiating with colleagues to change or delegate situations that are a source of stress.

Palliative strategies are less direct. Principals who use palliative mental strategies (Kyriacou, 2001) may reanalyze or reappraise a stressful situation to make it seem less stressful. Palliative physical strategies involve activities that help principals relax by relieving built-up tension and anxiety.

Locus of Control. We believe an individual's locus of control influences the relationship between source of stress, coping strategy, and mental well-being. That is, individuals who perceive stress as external will be more likely to use direct action strategies that focus on altering stressful situations. In contrast, individuals who perceive the causes of stress as internal may adopt palliative coping strategies. Most of us have discovered that personal coping strategies that involve positive and direct action are the most successful.

Cognitive and Physical Strategies. Cognitive coping strategies include positive thinking, setting realistic expectations, pragmatism, and blocking out the negative. Physical coping strategies may be active (recreation, sports, and general exercise) or more passive (listening to music, watching television, reading). We believe that the most effective form of stress management is physical exercise. Other physical outlets that allow individuals to distance themselves from their jobs include routines requiring little thought, such as walking the dog, doing housework, and mowing the lawn.

Here are additional coping strategies to remember:

- Keep problems in perspective.
- Avoid confrontations whenever possible.
- Try to relax before, during, and after work.
- Become a problem solver and work with teams.
- Express your feelings to others and be honest.
- Create a healthy lifestyle.
- Prioritize and keep priorities in sight.
- Learn and remember your own limitations.

These strategies highlight the importance of recognizing your own perceptions of stress and using individual action to create a virtuous circle whereby the same "objective" stressor can seem less demanding. Possible, but more easily said than done!

Response to Change

Take a few seconds and complete the following statements:

1. Stress is _____

2. When I am stressed, I feel _____

Perhaps you completed the first statement by adding one word such as "painful," "frustrating," or "necessary." You may have elaborated with a more detailed statement such as "Stress is manageable." In the second sentence, you may have concluded that when you are stressed you feel "anxious" or "upset." Whatever your response was, it probably centered around how your body reacts to change.

Stress occurs when your body reacts to change. These changes can be physical, mental, or emotional, and they can be positive or negative. Stress may occur as a result of positive change, such as buying a new house, receiving a job promotion, or adding a new child to the family. Stress will also occur as a result of negative change, such as the death of a loved one, uncertainty with regard to priorities or role, or financial difficulties.

The results of positive stress and negative stress are different. Consider a job promotion. Although you are excited about the promotion, the resulting change—more responsibility, higher expectations from your boss—will cause stress. If you view this change as positive, the body will accept or adapt to the change, thereby limiting or decreasing the problems that are associated with the stress. In contrast, consider what might happen if you were fired from your job. Your body reacts to this kind of change negatively. You feel defeated, isolated, alienated, angry. You become concerned about financial insecurity and possible loss of personal property. The effects of this kind of stress can build up over time if your body fails to accept or adapt to the kinds of changes required of you. The result may be health problems such as the following:

1. headaches	5. impotence
2. ulcers	6. depression
3. back pain	7. weight loss or gain
4. dizziness	8. insomnia

Helping Your Body Adapt to Change. Your negative stress can become positive stress and vice versa. You can turn your job loss into a promotion by moving to a different or better school, district, or position; or by becoming an educational consultant; or by starting your own successful business. You can turn a 30-minute traffic jam (a classic external stressor that creates internal stressors like frustration and anger) into an opportunity to sit quietly and listen to music, to dictate a letter, or even to skim a journal article (carefully!), all activities that will help you feel productive rather than stressed.

Stress Capacity

Stress capacity is the amount of stress an individual can absorb before a negative reaction occurs. Some people can handle a mishap by laughing it off. Others in the same situation may become ill or kick the dog or drive to the closest bar for a drink. It is impossible to list all of the factors that influence an individual's stress capacity—personality, personal and professional security, self-concept, physical condition, genetics, past successes or failures, relevance, attitude, sleeping and eating patterns (the list is endless)—but most of us recognize the limits of our stress capacity by using the "final straw" concept.

The damaging influence of stress appears to occur when the stress capacity is exceeded. The longer it is exceeded, the greater the damage. But the body has amazing recuperative abilities. By checking your present stress capacity, you can determine whether you need to make changes in your life to reduce stress.

Checklist 3.1

Identifying Your Personal Stress Level

Take a few moments to answer the following personal questions with a "yes" or "no."

1. In the past two months, has a family member told you that you appeared "uptight," "stressed out," or "tired"? Yes _____ No _____

2. In the past two months, has a friend told you that you appeared "uptight," "stressed out," or "tired"? Yes _____ No _____

3. In the past two months, have more than three individuals told you that you appeared "uptight," "stressed out," or "tired"? Yes _____ No _____

4. Do you find yourself more argumentative, snappy, or "short" with family or friends? Yes _____ No _____

5. Do friends or family members appear shocked, surprised, or become emotional with your actions or reactions to events, problems, conversations, and so on? Yes _____ No _____

6. If the answer to question 5 is
"yes," is this more than they did
two months ago?   Yes _____   No _____

7. Do you feel you have surpassed
your stress capacity or your ability
to handle stress?   Yes _____   No _____

8. Do you feel depressed, anxious,
or stressed?   Yes _____   No _____

9. Do you drink alcohol or take
anti-anxiety medication to relax?   Yes _____   No _____

10. If you answered "yes" to question 9,
have these actions increased in
frequency in the past two months?   Yes _____   No _____

To score your answers, count the questions to which you responded
"yes." Multiply the number of "yes" answers by 2.

Your score: _____

Checklist 3.2

Identifying Your Leadership Stress Level

Complete the following leadership questions by checking "yes" or "no."

1. In the past two months, have
colleagues, superiors or faculty,
and/or office employees stated that
you look tired or appear stressed?   Yes _____   No _____

2. In the past two months, have more
than three individuals stated that you
look tired or appear stressed?   Yes _____   No _____

3. Have you received additional duties
at work that require more time, detail,
and responsibility?   Yes _____   No _____

4. Do you feel that you have a time management problem at school? Yes _____ No _____

5. Do you find yourself daydreaming or romanticizing about times that were not as demanding or which required less time and gave you more freedom? Yes _____ No _____

6. If the answer to question 5 is "yes," has this increased in frequency in the past two months? Yes _____ No _____

7. Do you exceed 60 hours per week in school/district activities? Yes _____ No _____

8. Do you prefer not to be bothered with people while at school/office, especially before and after school? Yes _____ No _____

9. Do you feel more depressed, anxious, or stressed when at school? Yes _____ No _____

10. Do you drink alcohol or take anti-anxiety medication before or during school hours? Yes _____ No _____

To score your answers, count the questions to which you responded "yes." Multiply the number of "yes" answers by 2.

Your score: _____

IDENTIFYING YOUR STRESS LEVELS

Let's begin with two questionnaires that will help you identify your personal (Checklist 3.1) and professional (Checklist 3.2) stress levels. Once you've calculated your scores, check them against the following scores of other educational leaders:

Your Personal Stress Level Score. Based on norms from educational leaders who have already completed this survey, a score of 0–4 indicates that you probably have no problems handling stress. A score of 6–14 indicates that you may have lifestyle issues (stress or other factors) worth further examination. A score above 14 points means that it's time for you to call your doctor to schedule an evaluation.

Your Professional Stress Level Score. Based on norms from educational leaders who have already completed this survey, a score of 0–4 indicates that you probably have no major problems at work affecting your temperament or stress capacity. A score of 6–14 indicates that you can be reasonably sure your work is having a negative impact on your temperament and stress capacity. A score above 14 points means that it's time for you to call your doctor to schedule an evaluation. We urge you to do so.

Understanding Your Stress Level

Many temporary or short-lived changes in your temperament can be simply the effects of mood, weather, or fatigue. More lasting changes or repeated changes, however, are likely due to stress. If you scored high on the personal stress questionnaire and low on the professional one, then you probably have a personal problem or situation that needs correction. Likewise, if you scored high on professional issues and low on personal ones, then you now have evidence of how things at work are causing you anxiety.

The most damaging situation exists if you scored high both in personal and professional areas. Don't feel alone. Most of us aren't mechanical enough to leave our personal problems at home when we go to the office or to leave our professional problems at school when we go home. Relax. Schedule an appointment with your doctor if you need to and then read on. Checklist 3.3 will help prepare you for your visit to the doctor.

Checklist 3.3

Identifying Your Stress Symptoms

Check all of the symptoms you have experienced in the last two weeks. If the symptom occurred three or more times, check it twice.

Symptoms

headaches	back pains	irritation
stomach pains	dizziness	sexual dysfunction
indigestion	extreme fatigue	insomnia
weight loss	depression	nervousness
weight gain	shortness of breath	tightness in chest

Count each check mark as one point. Add up your points.

Your score: _____

Your Stress Symptom Score. Based on norms from educational leaders who have already completed this survey, a score of 0–3 indicates that you probably don't have a problem managing stress symptoms. A score of 4–8 indicates that you could benefit from seeing your doctor to discuss a stress management program. A score of 9–15 indicates that your stress capacity has been exceeded and you're at risk of serious health problems. It's definitely time to call your doctor to schedule an evaluation.

It is important to mention here that many of the symptoms in this questionnaire may have causes other than stress. Many minor and major illnesses are accompanied by these symptoms. But it is also true that symptoms of serious illness, such as hypertension, can be worsened by stress. If you are experiencing symptoms or pain, then you need to see a doctor.

> Maximum Joy
>
> Although most would like to believe that money and looks make us happy, research has shown that the real key to happiness lies within ourselves. Half of our happiness depends on our genetic "set point," or our usual level of comfort, and about 40% is influenced by what we do deliberately to make ourselves happy (Malin, 2003).

REDUCING STRESS LEVELS

Throughout this book, we will offer many strategies for *preventing* stress: managing personal and professional priorities; managing time bandits like perfectionism, procrastination, and the inability to say "no"; and developing programs for healthy physical activities and nutrition. But at some point, prevention won't be enough and you will need to turn to strategies for *reducing* stress. Read on.

Meet Walter: A New Assistant Superintendent

Walter, a prosperous middle school supervisor, was recently promoted to assistant superintendent for curriculum and instruction. Walter was most successful during the past eight years as a middle school supervisor, and many believe that his promotion is overdue. In his new position, Walter has discovered that his superintendent is ineffective and lacks organization, and now that Walter is around, the superintendent has delegated most problem areas to him, many of which are outside his job description.

Although Walter is an excellent problem solver, his boss is receiving most of the glory, including financial rewards. Walter is averaging 70+ hours per week on the job and has never taken an appropriate lunch break. He is no longer able to attend his son's high school basketball games, and in addition to his 70+ hours at the office, Walter brings district work home daily. His wife, Ellen, has become distant and goes out socially on her own.

Walter has periods of insomnia, a nagging headache that occurs almost daily, stomach problems compounded by daily periods of indigestion, and an unexplained weight loss of 15 pounds. Friends say he is nervous, appears fatigued all of the time, and is easily irritated. During the last month, Walter has become apathetic, missed work, and slumped into a depressed state.

Walter's Stress Symptoms

Walter checked the following symptoms on his questionnaire:

Walter's Symptoms		
✓✓ Headaches	Back pains	✓✓ Irritation
✓✓ Stomach pains	Dizziness	Impotence
✓✓ Indigestion	✓✓ Extreme fatigue	Insomnia
✓ Weight loss	✓ Depression	✓✓ Nervousness
Weight gain	Shortness of breath	Tightness in chest

Walter's score: <u>14 points</u>

Walter has problems. He needs to reassess his priorities, and according to our stress symptom scale, he probably needs professional medical assistance. Walter needs to think about whether he should leave the district office and return to a school site as a principal or find some other way to use his leadership skills at work. We hope he can rescue his marriage before it's too late. Although Walter may be able to make these improvements on his own, he would benefit from a support system and the appropriate professional guidance.

Choosing Adaptive Behaviors

You have three choices when thinking of ways to improve your life.

1. You can accept things as they are and not make needed changes.

2. You can quit work and become a monk or hermit.

3. You can modify your situation, make appropriate changes, and improve the quality of your life.

Prevention is the best change, but when prevention doesn't work you'll need to turn to adaptive behaviors and activities. During adaptive activities, your stress level is lowered, you experience no negative or harmful side effects, and you may experience

Figure 3.2   Basic Stress Reduction Activities

I. Exercises

- Walking
- Running
- Jogging
- Swimming
- Bicycling
- Tennis
- Dancing
- Martial Arts

II. Sports/Recreation

- Softball
- Bowling
- Badminton
- Boating
- Skiing
- Camping
- Horseback Riding
- Hiking

III. Musical

- Listening to Music
- Singing
- Playing a Musical Instrument

IV. Games

- Card Games
- Computer Games
- Board Games

additional positive side effects. Examples of adaptive behaviors are walking, swimming, most forms of exercise, listening to music, and biofeedback. In addition to lowering stress levels, these activities can help you improve strength, flexibility, breathing, heart rate, and overall fitness.

Quite the opposite of adaptive behaviors are maladaptive behaviors. Maladaptive behaviors are activities you can use to lower stress levels but which have harmful or negative side effects. Examples are inappropriate use of alcohol, abuse of tranquilizers, smoking, and excessive eating.

To be effective, you should select adaptive behaviors that you find enjoyable. Figure 3.2 offers a list, by no means complete, of basic activities that will allow you to adapt your behavior to lower your stress level.

Figure 3.2 offers just a sampling of activities to think about. Experiment with several of them until you find what is right for

Figure 3.3   Doing the plank.

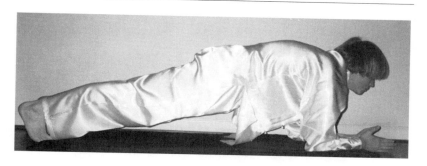

Figure 3.4   Find a serene yoga haven.

Figure 3.5   Visit a penguin colony in Argentina.

you, but remember that a stress reducing activity for one person (jogging, perhaps) may be a negative stressor for another. Can't find anything yet? Well, here comes a mixed bag of 10 more stress relievers.

More Stress Relievers

1. Do "the plank." This exercise enhances your balance and improves abdominal strength. Get into a push-up position by placing your forearms on the floor with your elbows under your shoulders (see Figure 3.3). Use your abdominal muscles to keep your hips up and your back straight.

HOLD. Do not let your hips droop to the floor. Concentrate for 15 to 30 seconds. Repeat three to four times.

2. Take a hot bath or spa session at 101°F for about 15 minutes. Add healing oils or minerals as desired.

3. Take a yoga tour or cruise. Go somewhere with great scenery, gourmet food, and numerous serene yoga havens (see Figure 3.4). *The Yoga Journal* is a good source to explore your options.

4. Shadowbox or punch a heavy canvas bag or speed bag.

5. Jump rope for two minutes without stopping.

6. Join a ballet or dance class.

7. Go rowing in a boat or try a rowing machine at your local gym. Indoor rowing machines give you a total body workout without the jostling of walking or running.

8. Go to the zoo or take a ride on a horse.

9. Take a Walk on the Wild Side (see Figure 3.5). Go snow skiing in Vail, go to Hong Kong and take a ride in a junk, visit an estancia (a working ranch) in Uruguay, visit a penguin colony in Argentina.

10. Be happy!

CHAPTER FOUR

Using Physical Activity as a Professional and Personal Coping Strategy

Figure 4.1 Physical exercise is a very effective coping strategy.

MANAGING PERCEIVED WORK DEMANDS

Perceived work demands are among the most common professional stressors principals must deal with. Coping strategies for everyday management of perceived work demands include

- learning to avoid procrastination
- learning to delegate
- learning to say "No" to tasks that take away from your professional priorities
- staying abreast of the latest curricular issues at the federal, state, and local levels
- staying aware of the structure, organization, and culture of the school

With the right attitude and perspective, principals can employ some of the best professional coping strategies even before the school year starts, including

- following good teacher recruitment policies
- asking human resource personnel to prescreen recommended candidates to avoid employer/employee mismatches
- setting realistic job expectations and task-specific requirements for teachers and school staff

School district leaders can and should also help reduce the gap between educational realities and the expectations of newly recruited principals by using realistic previews as a recruitment tool. Similar steps should be applied in the selection process. A superintendent or human resource officer might analyze carefully the tasks involved in the day-to-day life of a principal in the specific district in order to identify which skills are actually necessary to perform job tasks, and then use this analysis to restructure the selection procedure. Effective use of accurate screening devices during the selection process, at both the school and district levels, helps insure a better fit between individual abilities and the school system's job requirements. A mismatch between needs and abilities due to poorly conceived or poorly executed recruitment and selection procedures can result in increased stress levels with negative effects on principals, students, and school systems.

Five Good Coping Strategies for Principals

1. Focus on the situation at hand. You will never be able to complete the task at hand if you are constantly worrying about upcoming events. Set priorities.

2. Use positive self statements and avoid thinking negatively. Think, "I'll just work through this one step at a time" rather than "I'll never get through this."

3. Develop organizational skills. Don't allow yourself to assume responsibility for everyone else. Delegate.

4. Set attainable goals with proper time limits.

5. Know your peak energy periods. Do you work better in the morning or afternoon? If you know your dry periods, and when you're less likely to be productive, you can schedule your heavier tasks accordingly.

FINDING TIME FOR PHYSICAL EXERCISE

In this chapter, we focus on physical activities that are recognized by health professionals as stress reducers when used appropriately and regularly. Select physical stress reducers that can be practiced before, during, or after school by taking into account personal preference, perceived effectiveness, availability of materials and space, and availability of proper training or guidance.

The Benefits of Physical Exercise

Physical exercise helps to relax the muscle tension caused by stress. Exercising also takes our attention and concentration off stressful thoughts and focuses us on the exercise and related skills. By increasing our exercise levels, we build up our energy levels, and that strengthens us to be more effective in other aspects of our personal and professional lives.

Exercises ranging from a simple walk around the school to running miles to prepare for a marathon can help to lower blood pressure and heart rate, increase endurance, improve mood, decrease appetite, increase metabolism, and reduce excessive biochemical activity in the immune system, as previously discussed. As our bodies become more resilient, stress becomes more easily managed simply due to improved conditioning.

Sustained exercise and the related increase in endurance are critical components of stress management. Endurance-creating exercise will help you to eliminate the physical symptoms that are identified with acute and chronic stress.

> **WARNING!**
>
> Before beginning any exercise program, it is imperative that you see your doctor for a physical examination and approval of your planned program.

Before Beginning

Remember, before beginning any physical exercise program, consult your health care professional. After your check-up or physical, follow two more guidelines:

- Make sure you have the proper dress, equipment, and instruction.
- Start and stay with a routine.

Some of the best activities to get involved with individually or with a partner, team, or club are walking, running, swimming, water aerobics, weight or resistance training, and dancing.

WALKING

Walking is the *best* exercise. Most principals walk several miles during a school day, but that kind of walking is not focused on relieving stress. Finding 10 minutes to walk around outdoors or in the gym during a duty-free lunch period is an excellent way to calm down and get refocused. During this 10 or 15 minutes, walk at your normal pace and slowly and deeply breathe in and out through your nostrils.

STRETCHING

Nothing is more immediately relaxing than five minutes of moderate stretching. While it may be hard to find a space for floor positions, standing positions can be done in almost any space.

> Research Note: Walk It Off
>
> A study of 109 people revealed that those who walked at least 9,000 steps a day—the equivalent of about 4½ miles—were more likely to have a healthier body (Yeager, 2003). Other studies have shown that short amounts of activity throughout the day burn as much fat as extended periods of exercise.

Standing Stretch

One very easy position is to stand straight and with feet together, then raise your arms and inhale as you lift. Hold for a count of three and then exhale and bring your arms down. Do this slowly and carefully. Repeat three or four times, if possible. When first learning this stretch, you may finding yourself lifting your heels off the floor, but it is important to learn to stretch as far as you can without lifting your heels.

Sitting Stretch

If you have a large towel or a mat, you can do a sitting stretch. Be careful and go slowly. Sit with your feet close together in a comfortable position. Remember that you are not doing a major workout here, you are trying to relax. Next, inhale deeply and bend forward S-L-O-W-L-Y, exhaling as you lower your upper body. Reach outward with your hands and stretch and reach for your knee or shin. Don't push hard and don't go as far as you can, just breathe and relax. Repeat three or four times.

Stretching for Pain Relief

If painful knees and an aching back are keeping you from working out, you may find stretching an ideal pain reliever. Strong muscles act as shock absorbers that help protect your joints, and strengthening the major muscle groups can help reduce or eliminate aches and pains.

Recommended exercises for pain relief include modified squats, chest fly with dumbbells, and toe stands. Over time you can add back extensions, knee flexion, and an overhead press (Stallinger, 2004). Be careful, though, because improper stretching can contribute to back pain. Muscles work in pairs, and when stretched together there can be unnecessary strain. Try active-isolated stretching, which helps to relax and isolate the muscle you want to stretch. Also, instead of holding each stretch for the traditional 10 or more seconds, perform short repetitions, holding each for about two seconds and trying to stretch a little farther each time (Wharton & Wharton, 2003).

Other stretching techniques that may fit your lifestyle (Wharton & Wharton, 2003):

- If you're working too much and not getting enough rest, try sitting in a chair and stretching your neck to each side. Follow by standing for chest and shoulder stretches to relax the muscles in your back.
- If your body aches all over after a big weekend of working in the yard or cleaning house, try lower back and hamstring stretches while lying on the floor. You might also try some inner and outer thigh stretches.
- If you're pregnant and your back is in knots, try calf stretches, side hamstring, and seated trunk rotations.

YOGA

Yoga is becoming increasingly popular in the United States. If you look you may find several different forms of yoga. Hatha yoga is the most popular and uses controlled breathing techniques, postures, and movements for relaxation and improved health. Some forms focus more on the mental and spiritual aspects of yoga, including meditation. Yoga means "union" of the mind and body, and people who practice yoga regularly discover improved health, reduced stress, and clearer thinking.

While many think of yoga as a New Age activity, the truth is quite the opposite. Yoga has been around for hundreds of years. Many consider that the great yogi Pantanjali, who lived around 200 B.C., was perhaps the first ever to write about yoga and the resulting benefits. Today, yoga instructors can be found in just about every city in the nation. Contact your local YMCA, community college, or community center to find a qualified instructor. You can also find training tapes and CDs, yoga camps and retreats, and yoga books and magazines.

Our Yoga Favorites

- You can learn more about yoga by reading the popular *Yoga Journal*, which is published six times per year (www.yogajournal.com).
- Videotapes and CDs with instruction by Patricia Walden and Rodney Yee are the best for the beginning student.
- We suggest visiting the Kripalu Center in western Massachusetts for a long weekend of yoga, spa treatments, and relaxation. The last time we were there, we also stopped to visit the nearby Norman Rockwell Museum to see some of the works created by the artist famous for his covers of *The Saturday Evening Post*.

PILATES

Pilates (pronounced pi-LAH-teez) was developed by Joseph Pilates, a German boxer who brought the exercise to the United States in the 1920s. Movements used in Pilates training focus on the muscles of the abdomen, lower back, and buttocks while using deep concentrated and correlated breathing. Five special pieces of equipment were developed by Pilates to help develop the muscles uniformly. The student or practitioner lies on a mat to do a series of stretches using the pulleys and other equipment to tense the muscles by using his or her own body and gravity to supply the needed resistance.

Pilates incorporates over 500 defined and controlled movements and incorporates elements of yoga and Zen meditation. Today the techniques used in Pilates can be learned through private instruction, fitness studios, and even hospitals. Physical therapists and sports teams use Pilates to improve strength, flexibility, and posture and to help prevent injury.

Most movements are done in sets of ten. Initially the Pilates method was designed for body alignment, injury prevention, and increased flexibility during physical rehabilitation, but the movement has now expanded throughout the country and is now promoted as a stand-alone sport.

Pilates intended his exercises to bring about a balance of mind and body. When done correctly, Pilates exercises strengthen the trunk and pelvis area and strengthen the lower back, which is frequently the site of stress-related pain. Pilates enthusiasts report relief from all types of neck and back pain, and some research has been published that indicates Pilates may also reduce arthritis pain. Pilates training often seems difficult at first, but with practice and qualified instruction, participants report improved posture, stronger muscle tone, and a reduction in stress levels after a few sessions.

Winsor Pilates, developed by Mari Winsor, is a modified version of Pilates without the use of equipment. The exercises include the roll-up, roll-over, single and double leg stretch, and the spine stretch forward, to list a few. We find 20 to 30 minutes with Mari Winsor's seven basic exercises to be excellent for burning calories and for reducing stress.

Caution

We caution individuals interested in Pilates to find a certified instructor who has completed the 600 hours of required training. We recommend that you begin Pilates training only with a qualified instructor. For more information, see www.pilates.com.

KARATE, KUNG FU, AND CARDIO KICKBOXING

Karate is a martial art that was brought to the United States after World War II. Origins are unclear, but many karateka—karate practitioners—believe that karate dates back a few thousand years to somewhere in India or China. Literally translated, karate means "empty hands," and it has evolved into a major sport throughout the world today.

Modern karate was developed by a schoolteacher from Okinawa named Ginchin Funakoshi, who later introduced it at several universities in Japan in the 1920s. Japanese karate evolved into several different styles based upon some of the first great masters' interpretations of what would be best. Japan has four major styles today: Shotokan, Shito-ryu, Wado-ryu, and Goju-ryu. "Ryu" means school. From these styles hundreds of other styles have been modified and developed.

Japan has not cornered the market on karate; China has several styles of Kung Fu, and Korea has Tae Kwon Do. American instructors have developed many variations and combinations to come up with American Karate. Perhaps the greatest martial artist of all time was a Kung Fu expert named Bruce Lee. Lee studied several forms of Chinese Kung Fu and boxing and later developed a style that went against any of the orthodox styles or systems, Jeet Kwon Do (the Way of the Intercepting Fist), and taught this art form until his mysterious death in 1973 while filming a martial arts movie in Hong Kong.

Today, you can study just about any type of karate that you wish. Unless you are interested in becoming a black belt, we believe most styles are basically similar. Karate students learn to use a series of arm blocks, kicks, punches, and strikes as a system of self-defense. In addition to self-defense, karate students use karate exercises for strengthening arm and leg muscles.

Students with the same level of ability (belt color or rank) participate in sparring activities known as kumite (KOO-Muh-TAY) for fun and competition. The softer side of karate is called kata (KA-tuh), which uses a prearranged sequence of exercises from simple to complex, performed in a dancelike manner. Funakoshi developed 19 such katas that are still taught in the pure form by instructors certified by the Japanese Karate Association. Prizes and trophies are awarded to the best performers (see Figure 4.2).

Closely related to karate, but somewhat more dangerous, is kickboxing. Kickboxing is usually full contact with a minimum of protective equipment. Cardio kickboxing is the variant usually used just for exercise, where only canvas bags are struck. While we don't recommend full contact kickboxing, the cardio kickboxing workout can be awesome for relieving stress and getting into shape.

If you decide to study karate, Kung Fu, or cardio kickboxing, we strongly recommend that you find a qualified instructor and check his or her credentials. Be sure to choose a class that focuses on karate for balance, breathing, meditation, and the physical

Figure 4.2   A perfect karate side kick can be used for fun,
competition, or stress reduction.

components that can help alleviate frustration, anger, anxiety, and unwanted pounds. Check out an instructor at the local community center or YMCA before shelling out $75 to $125 per month in fees. Try working out in loose fitting clothes, such as a jogging or sweat suit, before you order a gi (pronounced GEE) or karate suit. Have fun, but be careful.

THERAPEUTIC MASSAGE

Various forms of therapeutic massage are available, including Swedish and Shiatsu. One very relaxing form of massage is effleurage, which uses extremely light touches to focus stress

Figure 4.3   Millions of people in Hong Kong and China practice T'ai Chi every morning as a way to achieve balance and peace.

away. For stress-linked pain, try investigating the scientific benefits of acupuncture and acupressure. And one of the most relaxing, and perhaps most healing, therapies today is reflexology, which focuses on nerve endings in the feet, with results that relieve pain and stress throughout the body.

ADDITIONAL PHYSICAL ACTIVITIES TO INVESTIGATE

Other stress relieving activities with a different twist include Judo, T'ai Chi Ch'uan, Qi Gong, Shiatsu, and Reiki. Books on these topics can be found at your local book store.

If you want an activity with a slow and graceful pace, join a T'ai Chi (TY-CHEE) class. T'ai Chi is an ancient exercise and art form that is practiced by millions all over the world as a way to achieve balance and peace. In Hong Kong and in China, you can find people of all ages practicing the art outside in the early morning.

CHAPTER FIVE

Desktop Yoga

Figure 5.1   Desktop yoga can be practiced at your desk, on your desk, with a class, or with a faculty group.

One of our favorite activities, desktop yoga can be practiced literally at your desk or on your desk. You can do these activities with a class. You can do these activities with faculty members. No special clothes or materials are required, and before you know it, everyone in the room can be doing these wonderful exercises.

CORRECT BREATHING

Before you begin, it is important that you breathe correctly for maximum benefits. Watch a baby breathe. A baby inhales as the diaphragm (even the stomach) rises or extends outward. As the baby exhales, the diaphragm lowers or comes inwards. That is normal breathing. As adults, we have changed that. We tend to breathe the opposite way. Well, time to change back. In desktop yoga, you breathe in deeply, RAISING or extending the diaphragm and stomach as you inhale, and LOWERING the diaphragm when exhaling. Let's experiment. Sit in a chair at your desk with your upper body straight and head up straight. Place your hand on your lower chest and inhale, pushing air into your lungs. You will feel your chest and stomach rise. Breathe in deeply and then exhale. Now you will feel your chest and stomach lower. Practice this several times. In fact this is an excellent way to relax. Just sit and breathe for four or five minutes. You will need to breathe in this manner when you do the desktop yoga exercises that follow.

To Learn More
See www.frazzledteachers.com to learn more about desktop yoga.

SITTING TREE

In sitting tree, sit at your desk (or on your desk with your legs crossed if you feel comfortable) to begin the pose. With your hands on your desk or by your side, inhale deeply. As you exhale, slowly bring your hands upwards until the palms of your hands touch. (Practice this so that you finish exhaling at the point your palms touch.) Your arms can be bent or straight. Sit in the tree position

Figure 5.2   Sitting tree.

and inhale and exhale one full breath slowly and then inhale deeply and exhale as you slowly lower your arms. Repeat two or three times.

TURNING BIRD

This exercise is most relaxing and can be great for students right before an exam. Sitting straight, as you did when practicing correct breathing, inhale deeply and exhale as you slowly lower your head gently forward. At the end of the exhale, inhale deeply and exhale slowly as you bring your head to a straight position. Next repeat by slowly dropping your head backwards as you exhale, inhale and return. Do the same with your neck to the left and then to the right.

If you get confused about breathing just remember that you inhale deeply while you are still and exhale as you move. You have it! Just be careful and do not push hard or bend deeply. Focus on your breathing. You are relaxing and not warming up for a marathon. Some individuals like to close their eyes during this exercise. You may find it more relaxing as well.

TIRED WARRIOR

Sit in your chair and inhale deeply with your arms at your sides. As you exhale, raise your arms upwards and slowly turn your head to the right. Hold and inhale deeply. Exhale and lower your

Figure 5.3   Tired warrior.

arms. Repeat, turning your head to the left. You can repeat this exercise two or three times on each side. Remember to exhale as you raise and lower your arms and turn your head.

DESK COBRA

This is a desktop variant of Rising Cobra. In Desk Cobra, place your head on top of your hands (left hand on top of right hand) and take a few slow breaths (Figure 5.4). Take a deep breath, and as you begin to exhale raise your head, move your hands apart flat on the desk, and stop at the end of your breath with your head extended backwards and your arms straight (Figure 5.5). Inhale and exhale for one full breath. Now inhale deeply, and exhale as you return slowly to the original position with your head on your hands. Sit and breathe two or three slow breaths and repeat two or three times.

Figure 5.4 Desk Cobra. Begin with your head on top of your hands as you inhale.

Figure 5.5   Desk Cobra. As you exhale, extend your head backwards.

NOSEY NEIGHBOR

There are two variations you can use here, either sitting on your desk or in your chair. In the first version, you sit on your desk (or on a towel or mat on the floor). Sit in a cross-legged position (or if you are a yogi, in a half lotus or full lotus) with your hands on your knees and your head turned slightly to the right. Inhale deeply and then exhale slowly as you turn your upper body (concentrate on your right shoulder and your head) and head to the right. As you are exhaling and turning, bring your left hand to your right knee and place your right hand on the desk behind you for support (Figure 5.6). Inhale and then exhale as you return to the original position. Then repeat the same movement to the left (Figure 5.7).

In the second version, you sit in a chair. As you exhale, you turn to the right. The left hand moves to your left knee and you can grasp the chair back with your right arm as you turn. Repeat to the left.

Figure 5.6   Nosey Neighbor. Turn your upper body to the right on the exhale, concentrating on your right shoulder and your head.

ALTERNATE BREATHING

This is an excellent sitting exercise. On the desk or in a chair, sit straight and place your right thumb and ring fingers on each side of your nose. With your right thumb, gently close your right nostril and inhale deeply through your left nostril (Figure 5.8). As you start to exhale, close your right nostril with your ring finger, release your thumb and exhale through your left nostril. Holding the position, inhale through your left nostril and as you begin to exhale, close the left nostril with your thumb and release the ring

Figure 5.7   Nosey Neighbor. After inhaling and exhaling as you
return to your original position, you repeat the same
movement to the left.

finger and exhale through your right nostril (Figure 5.9). Repeat
several times.

If you get lost, remember that you inhale through one nostril,
close that nostril and exhale through the other, then inhale
through the same nostril you just used for the exhale.

HEAD ROTATION

This exercise is similar to Turning Bird in that the positioning
is the same, but the movement is flowing and continuous. This
movement is great when you are tired and need a refreshing boost.
You will be making a circle with your head around and over your
shoulders and back.

Figure 5.8   Alternate Breathing. Begin by closing your right nostril and inhaling deeply through your left nostril.

Figure 5.9   Alternate Breathing. After inhaling, close your left nostril, exhale through your right nostril, and then keep your right nostril open as you begin the inhale-exhale sequence again.

Figure 5.10 Head Rotation. Begin by sitting up straight. Inhale deeply.

Figure 5.11 Head Rotation. Exhale slowly as you lower your head gently forward.

Figure 5.12 Head Rotation. Continue the exhale and the movement without stopping as you move your head upwards and to your left.

Figure 5.13 Head Rotation. Continue the exhale as you drop your head behind you and to your right. Keep exhaling until you return to the first position (Figure 5.10).

Sitting straight as you did in Turning Bird (Figure 5.10), inhale VERY deeply and then exhale SLOWLY as you slowly lower your head gently forward (Figure 5.11), then continue the movement without stopping as you move your head upwards and to your left (Figure 5.12). Continue your exhalation as you drop your head behind you and then to the right (Figure 5.13). Keep exhaling until you return to the first position (Figure 5.10). Rest. Take a deep breath and repeat.

You may want to do this two or three times, but do it slowly and gently stretch a bit further as you circle. Remember, there is only one complete breath per full circle. Inhale before you start and exhale as you rotate.

LEG WRAP

This is a different type of exercise in that you stand, but hold on to your desk for support (Figure 5.14). Inhale deeply and then slowly start bending your body forward. Taking your left hand like a snake (Figure 5.15), come inside (to the right of your left ankle) and move around to grab your ankle on the left side. If you can only reach your knee or upper leg, that is acceptable (Figure 5.16). Eventually you will be able to reach your ankle and perhaps even move your hand out beyond your toes. Exhale while you are moving down and be sure to hold on to the table. When you stop, take a deep breath and then exhale and retrace your movement back to a standing position. Repeat two or three times, change legs, and repeat.

A goal to aim for is using your right arm as well and moving away from the desk as support (Figure 5.17). Do this only once you get more comfortable. For another variation, as you exhale and grab the left ankle, stop, take a deep breath, exhale, and raise the RIGHT arm straight up with the palm facing behind you. Extend, holding with the left hand and stretching with the right arm. Take a deep breath, and come up as before letting both arms drop to your side.

As you become expert at this exercise, add a head turn to the pose. Once you have your left ankle wrapped with your left hand and your right arm fully extended, HOLD, take a deep breath, exhale while turning your head up and to the right looking at

Figure 5.14 Leg Wrap. This is a standing exercise, but hold on to a table or your desk for support.

your right hand. HOLD, deep breath, HOLD, exhale, HOLD, then exhale returning the head downwards. Hold and inhale and then exhale, and bring the body up and the arms to each side. Repeat once and do the same with the right leg.

SITTING DOG AND SITTING CAT

Think of a dog standing on all fours. As the dog looks up, the head is up while the body is straight. Now, sit at a table or a desk and reach forward with your hands flat on the desk. You can either sit or keep your feet on the floor. Breathe in deeply, and as

Figure 5.15 Leg Wrap. On the inhale, bend forward, and using your
left hand like a snake, bring your hand to the right of
your left ankle and grab your ankle on the left side.

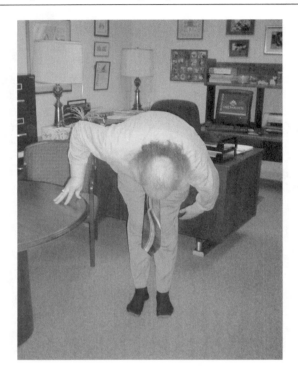

you exhale raise your head up and straighten the arms (Figure
5.18). Hold, inhale, then exhale, and return to the original position. Do this a few times and then move from Sitting Dog into
Sitting Cat.

Start in Sitting Dog with head straight. As you exhale, raise
your head and straighten your arms, exhaling as you go. Then
take a quick breath, exhale, and drop your head, lift your shoulders and pull in your hips (Figure 5.19). Hold. Take a deep breath,
exhale, and reverse your movement going back into Sitting Dog.
To do this, slowly exhale, push your head up, straighten your
arms, and lift your hips and stretch. Hold, inhale, then exhale, and
go back into Sitting Cat.

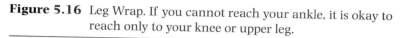

Figure 5.16 Leg Wrap. If you cannot reach your ankle, it is okay to reach only to your knee or upper leg.

Repeat this sequence several times. It feels great for your back and leaves you loose and relaxed, but PLEASE do these movements slowly. Never rush or jerk yourself into these positions.

CROSS-LEGGED MEDITATION

With practice, you may be able to meditate while sitting on a sturdy table or desk, but beginners should use a blanket or towel on the floor for safety.

Begin by simply crossing your legs in a comfortable position and dropping your arms on your legs. Some people like to lower their head slightly, but we think it is better to sit tall with the head up (Figure 5.20). Once you are in this position, breathe regularly,

Figure 5.17 Leg Wrap. A goal to aim for is using both arms and
moving away from the desk for support.

and gradually slow the pace of your breathing. Close your eyes
and try to "empty your mind" or think of nothing while you
breathe. When a thought enters your mind, try to concentrate
more on your breathing.

Another alternative is to keep your eyes open and concentrate
on a visible object or spot on the wall. Don't think about the spot,
just focus on it, lose yourself, and keep breathing.

Meditate for five or six minutes or until you feel your legs
begin to cramp. Extend your time with daily practice, aiming for
20 minutes twice a day, in the morning and in the evening.
Meditation helps you both mentally and physically.

Figure 5.18 Sitting Dog. On the exhale, raise your head up and straighten your arms.

Figure 5.19 Sitting Cat. On the exhale, drop your head, lift your shoulders, and pull in your hips.

Figure 5.20 Meditation. Cross your legs in a comfortable position, drop your arms on your legs, breathe regularly and slowly, and "empty your mind."

DESK REST

This is one of the best exercises to use to end a desk yoga session. Or, if you have time to do just one exercise while at school, do this one. Clear a space on your desk or at a table. Just move things out of the way. Trust me, they will all still be there when you are finished.

Choose the variation that is most comfortable for you. In version one, simply stand up straight and drop your body and arms limply over the desk or table. Put your head to either side and just melt. Breathe slowly and try to freeze your thoughts for a few

Figure 5.21 Desk Rest. Choose the variation that is most comfortable for you. Breathe slowly, freeze your thoughts, and melt into your desk.

minutes. A second version is to sit and then drop your body and arms over the table or desk (Figure 5.21). A third version starts with you on the desk with your face to one side. Then inhale deeply, lift your head slightly, and turn as you exhale, putting your face to the other side. Rest. Take a few breaths and then turn your face back to the original position. Remember to exhale only while moving. Finish with just a moment of total melting into the desk. RELAX!

CHAPTER SIX

Immediate Stress Reducers

Figure 6.1   Your stress reduction plan will work if you include prevention, leisure and recreation, physical activity, and immediate stress reducers.

P revention is the best medicine. But even with prevention, leisure and recreation, and physical activity, you may not escape all negative stress. When you find yourself in a situation that suddenly increases your stress level, exceeds your stress capacity, or leaves you feeling as though you are going to lose control—for example, during a lesson or after dealing with a difficult parent or a discipline problem—then you are going to need an immediate stress reducer.

In these situations, we recommend the Squeezer, the Breather, or the Calmer. You can use these activities to help you regain immediate control as needed, and you can also use them in more depth or for a longer time period before and after school as well. Of course, these activities will not take you from a high and possibly explosive state to a completely calm state of nirvana, but they will keep you from exploding, screaming, shouting, or walking away. They will help you regain your composure and assist in your maintaining a high level of physical, mental, and emotional control.

THE SQUEEZER

The Squeezer can be done as follows:

1. In a sitting or standing position, drop your arms heavily downward and let them just hang by your sides.

2. Squeeze your hands as though you have a lemon in each hand. Squeeze the imaginary lemons simultaneously, holding the squeeze firmly for a count of three. Repeat twice.

3. Now squeeze your hands and tighten the arms up to the shoulder level. Hold for a count of three.

4. Repeat two or three times.

You can become an expert in a few weeks and be able to squeeze and lock all muscles in your body for a count of three. As a form of deep muscle relaxation, the Squeezer allows the muscles to contract and relax, thus bringing you relief from stress. The more you practice this technique and the more of your body you include in this exercise, the greater the stress relief.

You may find the Squeezer is an important addition to your stress management program, especially useful before and after stressful meetings, confrontations with employer or employees, and physical or mental contests. Most

> **Caution**
>
> The Squeezer is a strenuous activity. If you have high blood pressure, a heart condition, or other chronic conditions, it is important to seek your physician's advice before beginning this exercise.

people prefer to do this activity in a private setting such as an office, rest room, or even a closet.

THE BREATHER

Some people prefer the Breather, which is easier to do than the Squeezer. The Breather can be done as follows:

1. Sit or stand quietly with your eyes closed. Hold your arms by your sides or in your lap.

2. Take a deep breath by inhaling through your nose. Hold for a count of three.

3. Push the breath out by exhaling through the mouth.

4. Repeat two or three times.

By itself, the Breather can be most relaxing. For maximum benefit, you may want to combine the Squeezer with the Breather. To do so, complete the following steps:

1. Sit or stand quietly with your eyes closed and let your arms dangle by your sides with no resistance.

2. Inhale through the nose while completing the Squeezer technique. Hold and contract and lock muscles for a count of three.

3. Exhale through the mouth while relaxing the muscles.

4. Repeat two or three times.

The Breather also can be used in crowded situations where you have no privacy, such as during a meeting or in a debate or argument. When this occurs, do the following:

1. Inhale lightly through your mouth, inhaling continuously for maximum capacity, usually to a count of four or five.

2. Exhale lightly, but immediately until the air is completely exhaled.

3. Repeat three or four times.

The success of the Breather is twofold: first, you are slowing down physically and mentally; second, you are focusing physically and mentally on the breathing and not on the situation, person, or event causing the excessive stress.

THE CALMER

Perhaps the most effective of all the immediate stress relievers is the Calmer. In the Calmer, you let your mental processes direct and control your body in removing stress. This exercise takes about 15 minutes and is best completed in a quiet, darkened room:

1. Sit or lie quietly with your eyes closed.

2. Memorize or record and play the Calmer dialogue.

3. Think of every direction in order as you remember the Calmer dialogue, or think and concentrate as you listen to the recording of the Calmer dialogue. *Do not speak or open your eyes during the activity.*

The Calmer Dialogue

(Deep breath, inhale, exhale)

I am sitting or lying quietly with my eyes closed. I am in control. I am in command of the stress I feel.

(Deep breath, inhale, exhale)

I feel a warm, comfortable feeling in my feet. My ankles, toes, and heels feel warm, as though I am in a warm whirlpool. The stress is flowing out of my feet. My feet are relaxed. I am in control.

(Deep breath, inhale, exhale)

I now feel the relaxing, warm, comfortable feeling flow from my upper legs. The warmth is now at my hips. The warmth increases as it flows down my thighs, my calves, my ankles, and my feet. With the flow there is a most relaxing feeling as though my body is in a warm hot tub or sauna. As this flow continues down my legs it pushes the stress from my hips, legs, and feet out of my body. I am relaxed from the waist down. I am in control.

(Deep breath, inhale, exhale)

Now I drop my arms limply by my sides. From my neck I feel a warm, continuous, and relaxing feeling radiating down my back and chest. It continues down both my arms to the ends of my fingers, down to my hips and legs, and out through my feet. I feel the flow of heat again, as though a warm shower is hitting me on the neck, down the chest and back, and down my entire body. I am completely relaxed from my neck to my toes. With each warm flow, stress is removed downward and out. I am in control.

(Deep breath, inhale, exhale)

Finally, I feel the warmth of the sun hit my head. The warmth is so relaxing. My breathing is slow. I am relaxing. As the warmth continues down my neck, back, hips, and legs, I demand any remaining stress to be completely removed. I am now in a completely relaxed state. I will remain here for a few more minutes. I continue to breathe slowly and calmly. I have controlled my stress. It no longer exists.

(Deep breath, inhale, exhale)

I am going to end this exercise, but I will continue to be relaxed. I know I can return to the Calmer whenever I become stressed again.

On the count of three, I will sit up straight and slowly stretch.

On the count of two, I will move around and become aware of my immediate environment.

On the count of one, I will open my eyes and be completely alert but extremely refreshed and relaxed.

Now three, two, one.

(Deep breath, inhale, exhale)

You should feel great at the end of the Calmer. At first you may want to record the dialogue and play it back during the exercise. This is an excellent form of visual imagery that you can expand to 30- to 60-minute sessions in the quietness of your home or office.

YOUR STRESS MANAGEMENT PLAN

All three of these immediate stress relievers can be major components in the overall management of your stress level. Although these are primarily designed for times when stress is overwhelming, you can incorporate them into your daily schedule. You will find the Calmer especially useful in preventing your stress level from building throughout the day.

Now it's time to put together your analyses from Chapter 2 (personal and leadership priorities) and Chapter 3 (stress levels) with the coping strategies, physical activities, and stress reducers that you've considered in Chapters 4, 5, and 6, and create a comprehensive stress management plan of your own. Planner 6.1 should help you begin that task.

Planner 6.1

Your Personal Stress Management Plan

A. LEVEL I. Prevention Techniques I Will Use

    1. _____

    2. _____

    3. _____

    4. _____

    5. _____

B. LEVEL II. Leisure/Recreation Activities I Will Use

    1. _____

    2. _____

    3. _____

    4. _____

    5. _____

C. LEVEL III. Immediate Stress Relievers I Will Use

1. _____
2. _____
3. _____
4. _____
5. _____

D. Situations, people, schedules, etc. that will assist me to be successful with Level I.

1. _____
2. _____
3. _____
4. _____
5. _____

E. Situations, people, schedules, etc. that will try to prevent me from being successful with Level I.

1. _____
2. _____
3. _____
4. _____
5. _____

F. Plan of action to correct problems listed in Item E.

1. _____
2. _____
3. _____
4. _____
5. _____

G. Situations, people, schedules, etc. that will assist me to be successful with Level II.

1. _____

2. _____

3. _____

4. _____

5. _____

H. Situations, people, schedules, etc. that will try to prevent me from being successful with Level II.

1. _____

2. _____

3. _____

4. _____

5. _____

I. Plan of action to correct problems listed in Item H.

1. _____

2. _____

3. _____

4. _____

5. _____

J. Situations, people, schedules, etc. that will assist me to be successful with Level III.

1. _____

2. _____

3. _____

4. _____

5. _____

K. Situations, people, schedules, etc. that will try to prevent me from being successful with Level III.

1. _____

2. _____

3. _____

4. _____

5. _____

L. Plan of action to correct problems listed in Item K.

1. _____

2. _____

3. _____

4. _____

5. _____

By having a workable plan, knowing your strengths, being aware of pitfalls, and implementing procedures to alleviate problems, you will master stress.

Whether you develop your plan in a notebook, computer, or on note cards, find ways to implement your plan, evaluate often, and make the adjustments that you want and need to make.

CHAPTER SEVEN

Arresting Time Bandits at Home and at School

Figure 7.1 Perfectionism, procrastination, and the inability to say "No" are the three major time bandits.

In our work in schools and universities, and in life generally, the three major time bandits or causes we have seen for time management problems are perfectionism, procrastination, and the inability to say "No." If all three of these general time bandits are in full operation in your life, then your time, stress, and priorities are probably seriously out of control. This can lead to a miserable existence, especially for a school principal or central office administrator.

PERFECTIONISM

While the old cliché "if it's worth doing, then it's worth doing right" has an element of truth to it, "getting it right" can drive extreme perfectionists to seek professional help.

Perfectionism, basically, is the desire to do something in a perfect manner. The perfectionist goes beyond the ordinary time or energy required to complete a specific task, never completely satisfied with the end product, regardless of how many times it has been revised. Ironically, some perfectionists are great procrastinators as well.

Many of us have perfectionist tendencies to varying degrees. For principals, perfectionism can become a general time robber, or it may produce several specific time robbers. For example, a high school principal who continues to redo the semester schedule over and over until he has a perfect balance of males and females in each class is a perfectionist who may also have difficulty moving on to his next administrative task. Most high school principals would set up a basic plan and then meet with assistant principals and counselors, delegating most of the detail work. Interestingly, the same principal who cannot complete a semester class schedule may have no problem completing the bus duty roster for teachers. At home, signs of perfectionism may be that the house always has to be in order, the car always clean, or one dirty dish must be washed. Perfectionism is a time bandit that can rob you of extra time, lead you away from your priorities, and create emotional stress.

Perfectionists have problems meeting their own expectations and even more problems meeting the expectations of superiors.

When external stresses increase—for example, an ultimatum to increase test scores or an annual progress report due for No Child Left Behind—that's when the perfectionist's expectations also increase as he or she creates additional work for self or others with delusions of exceeding requirements that may already be excessive. Failure to exceed requirements causes the perfectionist to feel great pain. If and when time limits run out and the perfectionist has not met his unrealistic expectations, he can be left feeling like a failure. When this occurs, the perfectionist often affirms, "Next time I will do it right," which sets up a cycle that reinforces the pattern of perfectionism.

Reality Checks

The best way to deal with perfectionism is to do more reality checks about perceived work demands. For example, if you need to write a report for an accreditation agency or a school report for the superintendent or school board, you can do a "reality check" with other principals or colleagues to compare your perception of the task with theirs. Assuming that you've chosen good principals for the reality check—professionals who know how to do what needs to be done—if you find that you are expecting to do much more than they are, this could be a sign that you have perfectionist tendencies.

> The Greatest Enemy
>
> Of perfectionists: the unrealistic agenda
>
> Of procrastinators: the unexpected event
>
> Of people who cannot say "No": fear

What you may need to do at this point is to realign your perception of the task with theirs before completing the task. You may find this difficult to do, but if you repeat your reality check and task realignment every time the urge hits you "not to let go," then in no time you will have readjusted the way you complete tasks.

If you feel depressed or unimportant or a failure after several attempts at reality checks and task realignment, then we urge you to consult an appropriate health care professional.

PROCRASTINATION

Procrastination is the time bandit that encourages you to "put off" a task, meeting, assignment, or lesson until a later time. Procrastinators usually take on too many tasks and many are perfectionists as well. Sometimes the procrastinator just does not want to do the task, which indicates an inability to say "No" to the task at the beginning. Other principals who procrastinate feel overwhelmed and may work around the task, secretly hoping it will just go away. Still other principals may seriously plan to do a larger task but decide to get smaller tasks completed before getting to the bigger item. In most cases, the small tasks get completed, but the major task gets further delayed.

The tasks that are most often put off to the last minute are the big items. For example, the superintendent requests your school safety plan two weeks from now. You are so busy just getting through the week that the first week passes, and on Monday morning you realize that the written plan is due this Friday afternoon. You rationalize that you will have time on Friday morning to do the entire plan, so you forget about it until then.

On Friday morning, you have the best intentions, but then one or two "unexpected" things happen. Perhaps the morning pep rally has gotten out of hand and you are called to the gym, or perhaps an irate parent is refusing to see anyone but you and the situation is getting ugly. What usually happens then is that by the time you sit down to start writing the plan, you realize the time allocated for the task is over, leaving you only half finished and missing your deadline. Or you do the plan too quickly, without detail, and the superintendent sees you on Monday and demands that the plan be redone correctly. These are just a few scenarios that may occur. Interestingly, many procrastinators remain painfully aware of the exact amount of time remaining to their deadlines but still remain subject to "unexpected" events.

Why Do You Procrastinate?

Probably, your reasons for procrastinating are similar to the general reasons listed above. One way to check your own reasons for procrastinating is by keeping a journal for two months and writing down your thoughts and feelings about things you are delaying. Be honest with yourself.

- Is it because you disagree with the task or assignment?
- Is it something you dislike?
- Are you letting the time bandit of perfectionism join forces with the time bandit of procrastination? Is it your intention to avoid the task? Do you want to do the task but feel too overwhelmed?
- If so, how do you feel about being overwhelmed?
- Are you capable of saying "No" when you are already overloaded?

If you stay loyal to recording your thoughts, after two months (perhaps before) you will see one of the above problem areas or a specific pattern emerge. Once you know why you procrastinate, you can begin to deal with your version of the problem. Along the way, begin breaking large tasks into smaller components. Try to complete the small parts in a timely manner, and before you know it you will have the big task completed.

One pattern we see frequently with school principals is procrastination because they are overwhelmed. And, quite honestly, the job of principal can be quite overwhelming. But often, overwhelmed principals are the ones who have not learned to say "No" to extra duties that are not required. Or perhaps they just think they can't say no.

INABILITY TO SAY "NO"

The third and perhaps most difficult time robber to battle is the inability to say "No," or to say it and really mean it. If you are the kind of person who worries about what other people think—what we call the "WOPT Complex"—then your priorities will suffer, and so will your time, and so will your stress levels.

The inability to say "No" usually results in a few patterns of behavior, whether the setting is personal or professional. In pattern one, you really don't want to do what is being asked of you, but you don't want to hurt someone's feelings or be thought of as uncaring. After you agree to do the task, you find yourself angry at being stuck with a project that you did not want to do and did not have time to do. So you complete the project by giving up priority time and increasing your level of stress.

The second pattern that emerges when you don't say "No" is that you find yourself procrastinating, unable to finish the task as you lose sleep or family time (growing stress problems in their own right), and then finally completing the task at the last minute by raising your own stress levels again.

The third pattern is accepting the task and then trying to find someone else during the eleventh hour to assist you to get it done. If you see yourself in this scenario, you are using other people's good will to get you out of a mess. Once they understand this pattern, the smart ones will say "No" to you next time.

Rules For Saying "No"

1. Respond politely with a smile, but state that you will be unable to accept the task.

2. If pressured, repeat more firmly, with a "No," that you are unwilling to do the task.

3. If still pressured, remind the person that you have already said "No" and that you will not be changing your mind. Then politely excuse yourself.

MANAGING YOUR PERSONAL AND PROFESSIONAL TIME BANDITS

The first thing we recommend is that you keep all of your activities (professional and personal) in one calendar, either electronic or a more traditional pen and paper calendar. We still know educators who use a notebook approach. The format doesn't matter. What matters is using your calendar appropriately.

The Advanced Planning Method

One great technique to manage time better at home is to mark personal time or family time in your calendar first. The Advanced Planning Method (APM) is just like planning your vacation. Most of us will mark our vacation and holidays off first thing when we get a new calendar. The APM approach is similar in that you go through your calendar on a monthly or at least weekly basis and mark periods of time that are for your personal or family time.

You probably listed more personal time or more time with your family as major priorities. If so, you have to make time for those priorities. Try to mark out 30 or 45 minutes per day for yourself and an equal amount of time for your family. As you learn to avoid procrastination, perfectionism, and the inability to say "No," you will have more time. You will also learn to label the more important priorities more quickly. Think right now how much time you truly have for yourself or your family—not just an appearance of time, but quality and quantity time. The APM will keep you focused!

The ABC Method

Another method is the ABC Method. To use this approach, think from a weekly perspective and pick a day, usually Friday or Sunday, and plan the week ahead.

Make three columns down the page. Label the A column as *High Priority and Urgent*. Label the B column as *High Priority and Important* and C as *Important and Not Urgent*. Make one list of all the tasks that have to be done during the next week and then categorize each item into one of the three columns. Be sure to check your priority lists from Chapter 6 and include those items in the appropriate columns. If your priority list reminds you that you want to walk for 30 minutes each day, then that should be a *High Priority and Urgent* task. If you put it in column C, it's less likely to happen.

Develop your own system using the ABC Method. You can add days across the columns or add specific times of day for specific tasks. Some tasks will already be scheduled, such as principal or board meetings. The real goal here is to reduce the number of *High Priority and Urgent* tasks by completing as many of them as possible while they are still *High Priority and Important*, before they become *High Priority and Urgent*. This cuts down on time problems, prevents stress, and provides you with the ability to make better choices and better manage your time.

Task Analysis

Another time management strategy involves doing an analysis of tasks that have to be done at home and then delegating these tasks fairly. Many principals end up leading all day and then coming home to clean house, prepare dinner, and run family errands. Divide these tasks among family members and then be firm in sticking to the plan. Remember, everything that you eliminate from your list of duties means more time for you. Other time management strategies follow below.

Reducing Driving Stress

- Give yourself more time to get where you are going (add an extra five minutes for every twenty minutes of expected time, ten minutes in heavy city traffic).
- Stay focused on driving and listen to soft music.
- Be patient and keep a good sense of humor.
- Don't use your cell phone while driving.

Working With Difficult Colleagues

- Inform them directly without being confrontational that what they are doing is bothering you or taking your time or causing you stress. Be assertive, but not aggressive.
- If the behavior does not improve, ask for a conference with the superintendent.
- Remember some people will never change. You may be the one who has to change your environment to get the peace you need.

Improving Communication Problems

- Really listen and try to understand the other person's viewpoint.
- Avoid "you" statements that can seem to attack.
- Watch your own body language; stay positive as much as possible.
- Be assertive without being aggressive.
- Learn to say "No" and mean it.

Additional School Time Savers

- Keep all plans written at least three weeks in advance.
- Leave later on Friday to get things ready for next week (good investment time).

- Use the ABC Method above and include instructional activities and meeting times.
- Propose in a principal meeting that meetings be held when input and interaction are needed but that informational items be shared by e-mail or newsletter.
- Ask for a moratorium on time outside of the school building during instructional hours.
- Ask for two weeks' notice for written reports that require data collection and analysis.
- Train your office manager in techniques for screening your calls and appointments.
- Set times for appointments in advance, and allow your secretary to schedule meetings with parents and teachers at these times. Schedule your own meetings only for emergencies.
- Ask for additional assistance in record keeping.
- Use parent volunteers for filing and doing clerical tasks that are not confidential.
- Stay with your routine; expect others you supervise to do the same.
- Seek creative ways to deal with noninstructional duties for your teachers.
- Aim to limit principal meetings to one per month.
- Recommend to faculty that they design or find an effective schoolwide discipline plan.
- Before agreeing to incentive programs, make sure additional help will be provided.
- Encourage teachers to use student-led conferences instead of individual or teacher-led conferences to reinforce how important time management is.
- Develop a buddy system with one or two assistant principals so they can cover duties for you when unexpected time robbers or personal emergencies arise. Make sure your assistant principals have plans in place to cover their own duties in such an event.

Keep adding to this list and share more with us and other educators on the exchange board that can be found at our website: www.frazzledteachers.com.

C H A P T E R   E I G H T

Using Nutrition to Support a Healthy Lifestyle

Figure 8.1 Lifestyle risk behaviors such as smoking, alcohol abuse, drug abuse, poor nutrition, and physical inactivity contribute to almost one-half of all deaths in the United States. With respect to improper eating habits, the problem of obesity is being debated as disease as opposed to just a behavior problem. As reported in *U.S. News and World Report*, the rate for Americans classified as obese has "quadrupled from about 1 in 200 to 1 in 50" since 1986 (Spake, 2004, p. 52). From the authors' perspectives, obesity is rapidly becoming an epidemic in the United States.

SCHOOLS AS A CULTURE
OF UNHEALTHY EATING HABITS

We know very few principals who eat a healthy well-balanced lunch during the school day. Unlike other professions, the principalship does not include a quiet, relaxing, hour-long lunch break. The lunch period, if it exists, often consists of time spent to scarf down something quick while simultaneously monitoring student behavior, listening to incessant chatter, and observing high volumes of social interaction. When principals do sit down to eat in the school cafeteria, usually it is to show support for staff.

According to the American Association of School Administrators, one of every six principals has high blood pressure, one of every two is obese, and one of every ten has a substance abuse problem. The reasons are many, but most are linked to schools as a culture of unhealthy eating habits:

- To battle midday fatigue, principals often reach for candy bars, cupcakes, or other sweets.
- At the end of the day, principals are often too tired for a nutritious dinner or exercise.
- On staff development days, staff breakfasts usually consist of doughnuts and coffee.
- Teacher's lounges feature daily sweets, birthday sweets, and holiday sweets.
- Fundraising events feature cakes, candies, and ice cream.

We gravitate toward those sweet, high-fat, empty calorie foods because our culture has trained us to choose them as a false reward for our hard work, and emotional stress triggers us to demand more food than we actually need. Those high-sugar foods do provide a quick surge in energy as an antidote to our fatigue. However, the deficiencies in essential vitamins and minerals contribute to ongoing feelings of fatigue, and coming down from a sugar rush can cause both irritability and further fatigue. With the constant stress, time pressure, fatigue, and poor food choices, it is no wonder that principals have so many health-related problems.

Research Note: Nutrition and Weight Control

Healthy eating plans for weight control and weight loss are controversial topics as research goes on concerning low-fat vs. low-carbohydrate foods, food pyramids, obesity, diabetes, and other topics. We will leave those debates to the scientists for the present. We prefer to follow a low-fat, high-fiber, and complex-carbohydrate eating plan for our health. As always, we strongly recommend that you seek the guidance of your physician. To learn more about nutrition, weight control, and physical activity, visit:

- The Food and Nutrition Information Network at the U.S. Department of Agriculture: http://www.usda.gov/. Specific information on the new Interactive Healthy Eating Index and Physical Activity Tool can be located by clicking the Food and Nutrition link.
- The Weight Control Information Network at the U.S. National Institute of Diabetes & Digestive & Kidney Diseases: www.niddk.nih.gov.

REDEFINING FOOD CHOICES FROM A HEALTHIER PERSPECTIVE

Good nutrition is essential for remedying stress, fatigue, and burnout. Preplanning enables you to make wiser food selections on a regular basis.

- Choose foods that are rich in iron, vitamin B, and folic acid: complex carbohydrate vegetables, lean proteins, apples, raisins, radishes, whole-grain breads and pastas. These foods can help reverse the effects of fatigue.
- Eat raw fruits and vegetables. They are not only quick and easy but they also provide essential nutrients and increase energy levels.
- Use the refrigerator in the teacher's lounge to store healthy snacks or a healthy lunch brought from home. That can help you avoid lounge temptations when you are feeling hungry, tired, and stressed.

- Schools are improving the nutritional content of the foods they serve. Plan in advance when you will eat in the school cafeteria and what you will choose.
- Focus on good nutrition for your staff as well as yourself. Poor nutrition has been linked to increased absenteeism and increased doctor visits. Look at good nutrition as a way to reduce absenteeism, increase productivity, and boost morale.
- Add physical activity to your day. When good nutrition is supplemented by regular physical activity, the impact of stress on the body and mind can be significantly reduced. As the American Dietetic Association points out, "The combination of nutrition and physical activity is also a primary strategy for reducing risk of coronary heart disease, hypertension, diabetes, and osteoporosis" ("For a healthful lifestyle," 1999, p. 994).

Schools have long had a culture in which high stress, unrealistic expectations, and overwork are the keywords for the day. Even though it is clear that it is time to shift to good nutrition and physical activity as keywords, few schools so far have implemented health promotion programs or taken the initiative to offer health education and proper nutritional information to educators.

In the big picture, a few dollars spent on educating principals about the benefits of good nutrition and daily exercise would positively affect not only their health and the health of faculty and students, but the final products of student learning. As educational leaders, principals can and should be leading the movement for everyone's improved health and quality of life.

IMPORTANT NUMBERS TO KNOW

Body Mass Index

Body mass index (BMI) is frequently used by health professionals to determine whether an individual is underweight, normal weight, overweight, or obese. These categories correlate to the individual's health risk status. For example, an individual with a BMI indicating "obesity" is at greater risk than an individual with a BMI indicating "overweight." One's BMI is determined by a mathematical formula, and we've provided a link to a Web site you can use to calculate your BMI.

> **Calculating BMI**
>
> To calculate your BMI, visit www.caloriecontrol.org/bmi.html
>
> A BMI of 18.5–24.9 is considered healthy. A BMI of 25.0–29.0 is considered overweight. A BMI of 30 or above is considered obese.

Cholesterol and Triglycerides

Cholesterol and triglycerides are blood lipid measurements that are used in screening for coronary artery disease.

Cholesterol screening is usually broken down into HDL (high density lipoproteins) and LDL (low density lipoproteins). Generally, total cholesterol levels below 200 mg/dl, with LDLs below 130 mg/dl and triglycerides between 40 to 150 mg/dl are considered within nor-

> **To Learn More**
>
> - about cholesterol, triglycerides, and blood glucose levels, visit www.niddk.nih.gov
> - about diabetes, visit diabetes.org
> - about hypertension, visit www.nhlbi.nih.gov

mal range. Normal HDL levels vary with gender, with normal male levels being between 35 to 65 mg/dl and female levels between 35 to 85 mg/dl. Lifestyle factors that have been linked to an increase in total cholesterol are a high-fat diet, lack of regular exercise, and stress. Factors linked to an increase in triglycerides include obesity and excessive use of alcohol. Unlike triglycerides, LDL, and total cholesterol—where increased levels should be avoided— raising HDL levels above 35 is good for you. Lifestyle factors that interfere with raising HDL levels include smoking, obesity, and physical inactivity.

Blood Glucose Levels

Blood glucose levels are measured in a fasting state, which means nothing to eat or drink except water or black coffee for 12 hours before testing.

A normal blood glucose result is between 60 and 110 mg/dl. This test measures how the body metabolizes carbohydrates. If the individual has a higher than normal fasting blood glucose level, further tests are required to check for diabetes or other conditions linked to insulin resistance.

Hypertension

Over 50 million Americans have hypertension or elevated blood pressure. Blood pressure is the force exerted to move blood as the heart pumps it through the vessels of the body. It is expressed as a ratio of systolic pressure over diastolic pressure (e.g., 120 over 70).

Hypertension is not diagnosed on one blood pressure reading alone since anxiety in the clinical setting of a doctor's office may cause blood pressure to rise. It is a good idea to check blood pressure frequently as that is the only way to diagnose elevated levels accurately. Hypertension is diagnosed when systolic pressure rises above 140 mmHg or diastolic pressure goes above 90 mmHg. Hypertension is linked to coronary artery disease, congestive heart failure, stroke, kidney failure, and other serious disorders. Early diagnosis and treatment are essential.

Balanced nutrition in addition to appropriate physical exercise, effective time and stress management, and an overall attitude of having a balanced and healthy lifestyle will help school principals to be more productive and be less frazzled.

CHAPTER NINE

What the Literature Says About Stress and School Leadership

PRINCIPALS

According to Clark and Clark (2002), learning must be the number one leadership priority of middle school principals. They contend that principals need to find more effective ways to lead and to organize their schools for learning by reexamining school values, school vision, instructional practices, cultural traditions, organizational structures, curricular decisions, and use of time and resources.

In a case study of four high school principals, Keedy and Simpson (2001) examined the reciprocal influence between principals and teachers involving the principals' priorities and teacher-identified school norms. They found that influence flowed from principals to teachers in all four high schools, but the teachers' influence on the principals was present in only two of the high schools.

In a survey of school principals from Indiana, disparities were shown to exist among rankings of perceived priorities and actual priorities. Several important conclusions emerged from this study:

- Principls felt that all the responsibilities of their jobs are important.
- No matter how much principals actually emphasized a task, they felt that they should be doing even more in that area.
- School climate was the highest priority among principals.
- Principals recognized the need for improving their time management.
- The numerous responsibilities of principals make the job tremendously stressful.

The researchers concluded that principals must first focus on the things they can control (Whitaker & Turner, 2000). Although it is obvious there is a need for more assistant principals and support personnel for the many tasks principals face, it is critical to address the areas that principals can control alone.

Two recommendations are offered: (1) Principals need to continue to develop, refine, and improve time management skills. Setting priorities is a necessity for administrator survival. (2) Principals need to consider the tasks involved to determine their importance. Recognizing which tasks principals must do and which tasks can be shared or delegated will not only alleviate stress for the principals but also empower their staff members.

Ripley (1997) discusses the tensions characterizing the principalship, including tensions of leadership (collaborative versus authoritarian, masculine versus feminine, instructional leadership versus managerial, and leader versus servant); tensions of need (one versus the many, professional versus personal demands, and teacher versus student growth); and social and cultural tensions (managerial versus communal vision, rhetoric versus reality, and stability versus change). He suggests greater balance is needed.

Drawing on the autobiographies of school principals, Brubaker and Simon (1996) propose guidelines that can help educators combat the occupational hazard of excessive stress. Each guideline is illustrated by vignettes from educational leaders who have learned how to avoid some thinking fallacies that could erode self-esteem and leadership effectiveness.

SCHOOL SUPERINTENDENTS

Chan, Pool, and Strickland (2001) examined the perspectives of 50 of the nation's best school superintendents to gain insight into their success. They used a self-designed instrument containing 38 quantifiable items in 5 sections: (1) the superintendent's background; (2) the superintendent's school district; (3) the superintendent's role; (4) the superintendent and his or her school board; and (5) the superintendent's leadership perspective. Surveys were sent to 50 superintendents.

Responses indicated that more than 77 percent had served as school principals at some point in their careers. No superintendent reported that he or she worked 40 or fewer hours; more than 85 percent worked 50 hours or more a week. Surprisingly, only 19 percent indicated daily symptoms of stress related to their jobs. More than 40 percent of the superintendents who needed to learn about school board/superintendent relationships went to the board chair, mostly using the telephone as their primary method of communication with their boards. Seventy-five percent indicated that the majority of their role was leadership rather than management. All responding superintendents rated their own overall performance as educational leaders as either exemplary (45.8 percent) or good (54.2 percent).

The superintendency is often described as an unpleasant, even impossible, job. Carter and Cunningham (1997) examine the changing conditions that affect the superintendency, present strategies for easing the burden, and offer guidance from practitioners.

The first part defines the superintendency and places it within its contemporary context. In the six chapters in Part 2, superintendents discuss the internal and external challenges that they face daily, such as negotiating community politics and controversy, responding to reform goals and mandates, coping with financial constraints, and resolving conflicts with school boards. The third part addresses what superintendents will need to do if schools are to achieve success in the future, such as building community alliances, developing district capacity, and motivating systemic change.

The final part provides a glimpse of what the new paradigm of education will look like and offers some strategies for creating 21st-century schools. Appendices contain information on superintendent responsibilities, an American Association of School Administrators (AASA) statement that outlines common ground for the improvement of public education, and components of the campaign for reform of central-office functions.

Richardson (2002) examined the evolution of the boundary-spanning role of the school superintendent and its impact on the ability to function effectively as educational leaders. This role, which is a relatively new development in the definition of superintendency, includes acting as a filtering agent controlling the flow of information in and out of the open and permeable boundary between the school system, the board of education, and the community. The various activities associated with boundary-spanning are also significant sources of stress.

Literature on the superintendency reveals boundary-spanning to be a major challenge to the position. To study the impact of boundary-spanning on the role of the superintendent, 149 Connecticut superintendents were surveyed via a mailed questionnaire, of which 109 produced usable returns. Data were analyzed qualitatively to determine types of major stressors and frequencies of incidence of each type. Sources of stress include politics, gaining support for budget, public criticism and expectations, the challenge of student achievement, negative press coverage, and the personal and professional toll exacted by a heavy workload. The primary recommendation, which holds policy implications, is the need to reexamine the position of school superintendent, paying particular attention to the boundary-spanning role.

The 2000 American Association of School Administrators Ten-Year Study of the American School Superintendent cites reports from superintendents that the superintendency is a very viable and rewarding career in public service. Despite this, they do indicate that a number of problems and troubling challenges exist; however, not so many as to seriously impair the educational process in their districts (Glass, Bjork, & Brunner, 2000).

The 2000 study results do not dramatically differ from those of the 1982 and 1992 studies. Both of those studies contained many questions comparable to those found in the 2000 study. These parallels have allowed the authors to analyze the 2000 data with a historical perspective. The 2000 sample is the largest of any of the ten-year studies, containing responses from 2,262 superintendents.

Of those reporting their gender, 1,953 were male and 297 were female, with 114 respondents identifying themselves as minorities. This report supplies information in the following subcategories: school board relationships, career patterns, superintendent tenure, stress in the superintendency, important problems facing superintendents and boards, satisfaction with the superintendency, community pressure/special interest groups, who influences the board, expectations of the superintendent by the board, communication with board members, female superintendents, minority superintendents, professional preparation, and superintendent salaries.

LEADERSHIP STRESS AND THE WORKPLACE

A survey of 575 spouses of Nebraska school administrators portrayed mounting pressure from increasing work demands. Fully 90 percent indicated that after-hours activities are exhausting and disruptive to family life. Other problems include dual home/office personalities, everyday job stress, unshared child-rearing responsibilities, and loneliness. Still, most spouses liked being married to an administrator (Bruckner, 1998).

Cooper (2001) offers tips on excelling as a leader by discussing changes that need to be made in order to reduce stress or shift tense energy into calm energy. He offers strategies for starting the day primed for calm energy; taking strategic pauses and essential breaks; and bringing one's best self home from the job.

From Great Britain, an article by Reed (2003) covers how workplace stress not only threatens people's health but can seriously undermine employee motivation and commitment. The author recommends "Four C's" for dealing with stress: (1) be Caring, (2) be Consistent, (3) Communicate, and (4) Clarify. He also suggests that a medical opinion (perhaps from an occupational health service) may be useful for identifying appropriate action at individual and organizational levels.

Thomas and Whan (1996) sought to identify stress when experienced by principals in their schools, to record the duration for periods of stress experienced, and to ascertain if and what particular administrative behaviors were associated with stress. Structured observation was used to record and time all activities of 10 elementary school principals in Sydney, Australia. Observed stressful behavior was confirmed by the use of a tissue perfusion monitor—a physiological measure of stress. All principals were shown to experience stress—some at heavy levels for extended periods. Eight categories of stressors were identified.

Research on teacher stress has become a major area of international research interest. Kyriacou (2001) reviews research findings on teacher stress and suggests five directions for future research: (1) monitoring the extent to which particular educational reforms are generating high levels of teacher stress; (2) exploring why some teachers are able to successfully negotiate periods of career reappraisal and process in terms of two types of triggers, one based on excessive demands, and (3) the other based on a concern with self image; (4) assessing the effectiveness of particular intervention strategies to reduce teacher stress; and (5) exploring the impact of teacher-student interaction and classroom climate on teacher stress.

Kagan, Kagan, and Watson (1995) conducted a three-year field study of 373 employees in the emergency medical service of a municipal fire department. A framework for defining stress and categorizing psychoeducational stress reduction programs was developed. The study determined the overall effect on job stress of seven psychoeducational programs: physiological (M), coping-with-people (A), interpersonal awareness (I) processes, and the four combination programs (A & I, M & A, M & I, and M & A & I). As well, improvements were found on standardized psychological instruments and on a job performance measure. The findings support the value of psychological instruments as job performance measures and support the value of psychoeducational training programs for preventive mental health in the workplace.

THE BIOLOGY OF STRESS

Clover and Haddy (2001) examined the effects of psychological stress on mental and physical health, including the response of humans to stress, the role of the central nervous system to stress response, and the interaction between stress hormones and immune system.

Novice school administrators find that demands for excellence have grown while budgets have shrunk. Kosmoski, Pollack, and Schmidt (1998) report on a study that examined the stress levels of beginning administrators. Two of the key questions for the study— Is the stress experienced by new school administrators manageable or out of control, and does the job put beginning school administrators at risk?—were answered by determining whether new administrators experience measurable changes in blood pressure. For the research, 43 beginning school administrators (25 females, 32 Caucasians, 9 African-Americans, 2 Hispanics) were monitored over a three-year period. Sixteen of the administrators were principals, 14 were assistant principals, and 13 were based at the central office. The study was conducted in a Midwestern megalopolis.

Results based on measurements of systolic and diastolic blood pressure indicate a significant main effect for systolic pressure and ethnicity. The average mean systolic pressure score for African-Americans exhibited a dramatic increase. There were no significant differences for systolic pressure between genders. An analysis of change in diastolic pressure yielded a significant main effect: all beginning administrators, both building-based and those in the central office, demonstrated a significant increase in diastolic pressure, suggesting that all novices were vulnerable.

Arnsten (1998) discusses the cognitive changes that occur in response to acute uncontrollable stress. Topics include release of neuromodulators called catecholamines in the central nervous system; stimulation of the amygdala and the prefrontal cortex; effects of catecholamine stimulation during stress; effects of exposure to mild to moderate to uncontrollable stress in humans, monkeys, and rats; and the stress reaction's value in evolution.

Booth (2001) examines the involvement of thoughts and feelings in physical performing activities in Auckland, New Zealand. The article addresses the susceptibility of stressed persons to upper respiratory infections, the congruency between structural transformations in the body and thoughts, and a study on the effects of social cohesion on human populations.

Key, DeNoon, and Boyles (1999) discuss the results of a study published in the *Journal of the American Medical Association* on the weakening effects of stress on the body's immune system. Topics include susceptibility to infection, reduced effectiveness of certain vaccines, and the role of cytokines in regulating immune response.

Bower (1999) discusses a study published in *Psychosomatic Medicine* covering subjects who felt unable to deal with life's stresses and displayed an exaggerated immune reaction that intensified physical symptoms once they had contracted a common virus. The article covers the rise in production of a chemical messenger known as interleukin-6 (IL-6), the research protocol and results, and the discussion linking psychological stress both to immune system change and verified disease outcome.

References

Arnsten, A. F., (1998, June 6). The biology of being frazzled. *Science, 280*, 1711–1712.

Booth, R. J. (2001). Mind-body common sense. *Advances in Mind–Body Medicine, 17*, 3.

Boreen, J., & Niday, D. (2000, October). Breaking through the isolation: Mentoring beginning teachers. *Journal of Adolescent & Adult Literacy, 44*(2), 152.

Bottoms, G., & O'Neill, K. (2001). *Preparing a new breed of school principals: It's time for action.* Atlanta, GA: Southern Regional Education Board.

Bower, B. (1999). Immune response may tie stress to colds. *Science News, 155*, 199.

Brubaker, D. L., & Simon, L. H. (1996). Private victories to enhance your self-esteem: A principal's guide to success. *Journal of Invitational Theory and Practice, 4*(1), 63–69.

Bruckner, M. (1998). Private lives of public leaders: A spousal perspective. *School Administrator, 55*(6), 24–27.

Carter, G. R., & Cunningham, W. G. (1997). *The American school superintendent: Leading in an age of pressure.* San Francisco: Jossey-Bass.

Chan, T. C., Pool, H., & Strickland, J. S. (2001, November). *Who's in charge around here?* Paper presented at the Annual Meeting of the Southern Regional Council on Educational Administration, Jacksonville, FL.

Clark, S., & Clark, D. (2002). Making leadership for learning the top priority. *Middle School Journal, 34*(2) 50–55.

Clover, R. D., & Haddy, R. I. (2001). The biological processes in psychological stress. *Families, Systems, and Health, 19*(3), 291–302.

Cooper, R. K. (2001). Excelling under pressure: Increasing your energy for leadership and innovation in a world of stress, change and unprecedented opportunities. *Strategy & Leadership, 29*(4), 15–20.

Educational Research Service. (1998). *Is there a shortage of qualified candidates for openings in the principalship? An exploratory study.* Retrieved July 18, 2003, from www.naesp.org/misc/shortage.htm

Ferrandino, V. L. (2001). Challenges for 21st-century elementary school principals. *Phi Delta Kappan, 82*, 440–442.

For a healthful lifestyle: Promoting cooperation among nutrition professionals and physical activity professionals. (1999). *Journal of the American Dietetic Association, 99*(8), 994.

Friedman, S. D., Christensen, P., & DeGroot, J. (1998). Work and life: The end of the zero-sum game. *Harvard Business Review, 76*, 119–129.

Furman, G., & Starratt, R. J. (2002). Leadership for democratic community in schools. In J. Murphy (Ed.), *The educational leadership challenge: Redefining leadership for the 21st century. One hundred-first yearbook of the National Society for the Study of Education* (pp. 105–133). Chicago: University of Chicago Press.

Glass, T. E., Bjork, L., & Brunner, C. (2000). *The study of the American school superintendency, 2000.* Arlington, VA: American Association of School Administrators.

Glickman, C., Gordon, S., & Ross-Gordon, J. (2001). *Supervision and instructional leadership* (5th ed.). Needham Heights, MA: Allyn & Bacon.

Gold, J., Thornton, L., & Metules, T. J. (2001, December). *Simple strategies for managing stress. RN, 64* (12), 65–67.

Goldring, E., & Greenfield, W. (2002). Understanding the evolving concept of leadership in education: Roles, expectations and dilemmas. In J. Murphy (Ed.), *The educational leadership challenge: Redefining leadership for the 21st century. One hundred-first yearbook of the National Society for the Study of Education* (pp. 1–19). Chicago: University of Chicago Press.

Goldring, E., & Rallis, S. (1993). *Principals of dynamic schools: Taking charge of change.* Newbury Park, CA: Corwin.

Kagan, H. K., Kagan, N. I., & Watson, M. G. (1995). Stress reduction in the workplace: The effectiveness of psychoeducational programs. *Journal of Counseling Psychology, 42*, 71–78.

Keedy, J. L., & Simpson, D. S. (2001). Principal priorities, school norms, and teacher influence: A study of sociocultural leadership in the high school. *Journal of Educational Administration and Foundations, 16*(1), 10–41.

Keithwood, K., & Prestine, N. (2002). Unpacking the challenges of leadership at the school and district level. In J. Murphy (Ed.), *The educational leadership challenge: Redefining leadership for the 21st century. One hundred-first yearbook of the National Society for the Study of Education* (pp. 42–64). Chicago: University of Chicago Press.

Key, K. K., DeNoon, D. J., & Boyles, S. (1999, August 9). Stress may increase susceptibility to infectious disease. *Vaccine Weekly*, 10–11.

Kochan, F., Riehl, C., & Bredeson, P. (2002). Professional development of school leaders in the 21st century. In J. Murphy (Ed.), *The educational *leadership challenge: Redefining leadership for the 21st century. One hundred-first yearbook of the National Society for the Study of Education.* Chicago: University of Chicago Press.

Kosmoski, G. J., Pollack, D. R., & Schmidt, L. J. (1998). *Novice administrators: psychological and physiological effects.* Mequone, WI: Stylex Publishing.

Kyriacou, C. (2001, February). Teacher stress: Directions for future research. *Educational Review, 53(1),* 27–33.

Lowery, S., Harris, S., Hopson, M., & Marshall, R. (2001, November). *Take this job and love it!* Paper presented at the Annual Meeting of University Council for Educational Administration, Cincinnati, OH.

Lugg, C. A., Bulkey, K., Firestone, W. A., & Garner, C. W. (2002). The contextual terrain facing educational leaders. In J. Murphy (Ed.), *The educational leadership challenge: Redefining leadership for the 21st century. One hundred-first yearbook of the National Society for the Study of Education* (pp. 20–41). Chicago: University of Chicago Press.

Malin, A. (2003, September). Maximum joy. *Prevention,* 117, 188.

Murphy, J. (2002a). Reculturing the profession of educational leadership: New blueprints. In J. Murphy (Ed.), *The educational leadership challenge: Redefining leadership for the 21st century. One hundred-first yearbook of the National Society for the Study of Education* (pp. 65–82). Chicago: University of Chicago Press.

Murphy, J. (2002b). *The educational leadership challenge: Redefining leadership for the 21st century. One hundred-first yearbook of the National Society for the Study of Education.* Chicago: University of Chicago Press.

Murphy, J., & Louis, K. S. (1999). *Handbook of research on educational administration. A project of the American Educational Research Association* (2nd ed.). San Francisco: Jossey-Bass.

National Association of Elementary School Principals. (1990). Over 50% of the principals in America will retire in the next ten years. *Principal, 70(4),* 65.

Peterson, K., & Kelley, C. (2001). Transforming school leadership. *Leadership, 30(3),* 8–11.

Plunkett, S. W., Radmacher, K. A., & Moll-Phanara, D. (2000). Adolescent life events, stress, and coping: A comparison of communities and genders. *Professional School Counseling, 3(5),* 356–366.

Pounder, D., Reitzug, U. C., & Young, M. (2002). Preparing school leaders for school improvement, social justice, and community. In J. Murphy (Ed.), *The educational leadership challenge: Redefining leadership for the 21st century. One hundred-first yearbook of the National Society for the Study of Education* (pp. 261–288). Chicago: University of Chicago Press.

Queen, A. (2002). *Responsible discipline: The RCM plan.* Charlotte: Writer's Edge Press.

Reed, J. (2003). Negative pressure. *People Management, 9*(14), 49.

Richardson, L. M. (1999). *Stress in the superintendency: Implications for achieving educational excellence.* Paper presented at the Annual Meeting of the University Council for Educational Administration, St. Louis, MO. (Eric Document Reproduction Service No. ED427421)

Richardson, L. M. (2002, April). *Boundary spanning in school leadership: Implications for achieving excellence.* Paper presented at the Annual Conference of the New England Educational Research Organization, Northampton, MA.

Ripley, D. (1997). Current tensions in the principalship: Finding an appropriate balance. *NASSP Bulletin, 81*(589), 55–65.

Rowan, B. (1995). Research on learning and teaching in K–12 schools: Implications for the field of educational administration. *Educational Administration Quarterly, 31,* 115–133.

Spillane, J. P., & Louis, K. S. (2002). School improvement process and practices: Professional learning for building instructional capacity. In J. Murphy (Ed.), *The educational leadership challenge: Redefining leadership for the 21st century. One hundred-first yearbook of the National Society for the Study of Education* (pp. 83–104). Chicago: University of Chicago Press.

Spake, A. (2004). Rethinking weight. *U.S. News and World Report, 136*(5), 50–56.

Stallinger, D. (2004, January/February). Pain busters. *AARP,* 69–73.

Steinberg, J. (2000, September 3). Nation's schools struggling to find enough principals. *New York Times,* 1.

Streisand, B., & Tote, T. (1998, September 14). Many millions of kids, and too few teachers: Across America, teaching jobs go wanting. *U.S. News & World Report, 125*(10), 24–25.

Stricherz, M. (2001, October 24). Despite retirements, 'Baby Busters' scarce in principal's positions. *Education Week, 21*(8), 6–7.

Thomas, A. R., & Whan, L. D. (1996, July). The principalship and stress in the workplace: An observational and physiological study. *Journal of School Leadership, 6,* 444–465.

Wallace, R. C. (1996). *From vision to practice: The art of educational leadership.* Thousand Oaks, CA: Corwin Press.

Wharton, J., & Wharton, P. (2003, October). Stretch away back pain. *Prevention,* 133–134.

Whitaker, T., & Turner, E. (2000). What is your priority? *NASSP Bulletin, 84*(617), 16–21.

Yeager, S. (2003, November). Walk it off. *Prevention,* 151–158.

Index